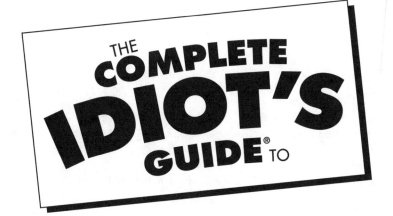

THE COMPLETE IDIOT'S GUIDE® TO

Car Care and Repair

Illustrated

by Dan Ramsey

ALPHA

A member of Penguin Group (USA) Inc.

ALPHA BOOKS

Published by the Penguin Group

Penguin Group (USA) Inc., 375 Hudson Street, New York, New York 10014, U.S.A.

Penguin Group (Canada), 10 Alcorn Avenue, Toronto, Ontario, Canada M4V 3B2 (a division of Pearson Penguin Canada Inc.)

Penguin Books Ltd, 80 Strand, London WC2R 0RL, England

Penguin Ireland, 25 St Stephen's Green, Dublin 2, Ireland (a division of Penguin Books Ltd)

Penguin Group (Australia), 250 Camberwell Road, Camberwell, Victoria 3124, Australia (a division of Pearson Australia Group Pty Ltd)

Penguin Books India Pvt Ltd, 11 Community Centre, Panchsheel Park, New Delhi—110 017, India

Penguin Group (NZ), cnr Airborne and Rosedale Roads, Albany, Auckland 1310, New Zealand (a division of Pearson New Zealand Ltd)

Penguin Books (South Africa) (Pty) Ltd, 24 Sturdee Avenue, Rosebank, Johannesburg 2196, South Africa

Penguin Books Ltd, Registered Offices: 80 Strand, London WC2R 0RL, England

Publisher: *Marie Butler-Knight*
Product Manager: *Phil Kitchel*
Managing Editor: *Jennifer Chisholm*
Senior Acquisitions Editor: *Mike Sanders*
Development Editor: *Lynn Northrup*
Production Editor: *Katherin Bidwell*
Copy Editor: *Susan Aufheimer*
Illustrator: *Chris Eliopoulos*
Cover/Book Designer: *Trina Wurst*
Indexer: *Brad Herriman*
Graphics: *Oliver Jackson, Tammy Graham*
Layout/Proofreading: *Angela Calvert, John Etchison, Trina Wurst*

This book is dedicated to Aaron Luedemann, my new son-in-law,
who exemplifies family values. Right on!

Contents at a Glance

Contents

Appendixes

Foreword

Although Dan Ramsey and I have yet to meet, we've been friends for years. It started when Dan volunteered to help with a newsletter I write for members of the National Association of Home and Workshop Writers. Dan and I are both longtime members of NAHWW. Dan is vice president, to become president in 2004.

When Dan asked me to write the foreword for his new book on car maintenance and repair, I was flattered. That is, until I saw its title: *The Complete Idiot's Guide to Car Care and Repair Illustrated*. Hmmm. I was like, *What's he mean by that?*

Then I got to thinking, Dan isn't accusing us of being idiots. It's a catchy title, that's all. Gotta get the reader's attention, right?

And attention it gets. This book is so profusely illustrated that Dan Ramsey could have titled his tome *Picture Book of Car Care and Repair*. The publisher confided to me that this is the most completely illustrated book they have ever done. On nearly every page are photographs. All of them are taken by Dan himself, especially for you. I think you could almost do the care and repair projects simply by following Dan's pictures.

You'll find the emphasis in this book is on things that *you* can do. The first chapter tantalizes with things you're going to learn about your car. Then you move step by step through the various projects. All the tools you'll use are covered. Along the way are precautions to keep you working safely.

The book makes the complicated seem easy and the difficult seem doable. In good training fashion, Dan tells you what he's going to tell you. Then he tells you. And then he tells you what he told you. This is a roadmap to easy understanding.

Dan's book tells where to get more information about your car. For example, the car's shop manual—that big, illustrated book that specifically covers your make and model of car—is critical to car fix-it. He also lists websites where you can learn more about your car (several actual sites are pictured).

As you go along, "Car Lingo" boxed features explain sidecar things about autos. Wise advice is included, like smart shopping for tools and parts. I especially like Dan's tip on installing longer-lasting platinum spark plugs in the hard-to-reach locations found on so many car engines today. Smart idea.

This book says "Yes, you *can* maintain and repair your own car." In fact, the book's theme is, "You can do as much on your car as you *want* to." On the other hand, sometimes you may not want to. For instance, in Chapter 14, Dan shows how to remove your car's dashboard. Now, I don't know about you, but I have no desire to remove the dashboard on my car. But perhaps someone does.

Well, I'm not the author, Dan Ramsey is. So I'd best get out of the way and let the expert take over.

But, as readers of this book, let's set one thing straight right from the start: We ain't no stupid idiots. We're just here to learn a lot about working on our cars. Cool thought.

—Richard Day

Founding Director and past President, National Association of Home and Workshop Writers; and former Consulting Editor, "Home and Shop," *Popular Science* magazine

Introduction

"Step 47b: Disassemble the fralater from the secondary modulon, ensuring that the stubenfels isn't damaged by adverse janonis torque."

Say what? Just give me a picture and some step-by-step instructions!

Today's cars are complex. They have ABS, DOHC, EFI, CV, PCV, and dozens of other acronyms. How can anyone except a certified technician (or a certifiable nut) try to maintain or repair modern cars?

The easiest way is to follow clear, illustrated instructions. *The Complete Idiot's Guide to Car Care and Repair Illustrated* offers hundreds of helpful photos and drawings that not only describe how cars run, but also show you exactly what to do when they don't run. You'll learn how to maintain your car without getting dirty. You'll also learn how to handle common repairs without a mechanic—or a cosigner. It covers domestic and foreign cars, small trucks, and sports-utility vehicles (SUVs) built in the last 25 years.

Specifically, *The Complete Idiot's Guide to Car Care and Repair Illustrated* covers maintaining, troubleshooting, and repairing your car from bumper to bumper, inside and out. It clearly describes and illustrates selecting tools and parts, changing oil, checking transmission and steering fluids, replacing filters, fixing body dings, and replacing your car's battery. There are dozens of illustrated step-by-step instructions for jobs that can save you hundreds or even thousands of dollars.

Who am I to show you how to care for and repair your car? Besides owning and maintaining dozens of my own cars over the past 40 years, I authored two successful editions of *The Complete Idiot's Guide to Trouble-Free Car Care* (Alpha Books, 1999) and numerous other popular how-to books for consumers and mechanics. And I called for help. ASE Master Technician Loren Luedemann helped me make sure this book is technically accurate and up to date. Loren is a full-time auto technician with loads of experience.

How to Use This Book

This book is presented in a very logical structure to make it easy to find things when you need them. Let's take a closer look at each part.

Part 1, "Your Car Illustrated," explains how cars work in general and how to understand *your* car in particular. It then helps you gather the parts and tools you'll need for maintaining and repairing your set of wheels. Then it opens up the wide world of resources, showing you how to get the information you need from the owner's manual and service manual written specifically for your car. Everything will be clearly illustrated in this book to make your car easier to understand.

Part 2, "Illustrated Maintenance," takes you to the next step. Whether you've never pulled a dipstick or you're already comfortable with tune-ups, this part offers something new and useful. More than 100 photos in this part take you step by step through all levels of common automotive maintenance from things you can do as you fill the gas tank to things you have to do only every other year. Expect loads of tips from our technician.

Part 3, "Illustrated Repairs," is for braver souls—and those who want to know what the mechanic is talking about. It offers dozens of illustrations and instructions for common automotive repairs. It covers easy mechanical (engine, transmission, suspension, brake, and cooling system) repairs as well as you-can-do-it electrical, body, and interior repairs. Tackle as many of them as you want and save some money.

In addition, you'll find a helpful illustrated Glossary at the back of the book that defines over 150 terms.

Extras

Along the way, practical sidebars will show you the safe and smart way to do things, define words and terms you may not be familiar with, point out any dangers or pitfalls, and give you other bits of helpful information. *The Complete Idiot's Guide to Car Care and Repair Illustrated* makes working on your car easier—and maybe even fun!

Technician's Tip

What does our ASE Master Technician have to add to the discussion? Find out here as Loren Luedemann shares tips and suggestions with you. Thankfully, you don't have to pay his shop rate for this valuable advice.

Car Lingo

What does *that* mean? Here you'll find a concise definition of important automotive terms in context. Also check the Glossary for more definitions and even some photos to make things more clear.

Auto Alert

Don't get hurt! Make sure you follow the cautions and warnings in these boxes and in your car's service manual.

Things You Should Know

Here are some other bits of valuable information that can help you take care of your car for less time and money.

Acknowledgments

Lots of folks helped me amass—and verify—the knowledge and tips offered in this book. I must thank them.

First, thanks to Master Technician Loren Luedemann of Ron's Muffler and Automotive in Willits, California, for his technical knowledge and his friendship. Both are top rate.

The folks at Little Lake Auto Parts (Dave and Cathy Bouthillier, and Dennis Nooneman) in Willits, California, were especially helpful and patient as I asked questions and took photos. Also, thanks to Ron Kendrick and James Walters at Ron's Muffler and Automotive for bay time and loads of practical advice for you, the reader. They're excellent technicians—and great guys!

Thanks to Steve Fowler, automotive instructor at Mendocino College in Ukiah, California, and Bob Bender, automotive instructor at Ukiah (California) High School, for auto component cutaways and valuable tips. And thanks to the staff at Coast Hardware in Willits, California, for preparing the oil filter cutaway in Chapter 7.

Additionally, thanks to the many folks who helped me develop my knowledge of cars. Rich Day, you're the primo auto how-to guy!

And a special thanks to Mike Sanders whose vision initiated this new visual step-by-step approach to practical how-to books. As always, a special thank-you to the Editorial Dream Team: Lynn Northrup, Susan Aufheimer, and Kathy Bidwell, who enhance my books with their valuable skills.

Trademarks

In This Part

Part 1

Your Car Illustrated

Honey, I shrunk myself!

Through the wizardry of digital photography, you will soon be climbing around inside your car's engine! You'll see what a combustion chamber looks like. You'll see how all the hundreds of components in your car work together to get you down the road. You'll discover how your car runs. Hey, it's really magic!

Most important, you'll find out how you can save thousands of dollars and keep your car years longer by simply understanding your car. Knowledge is power.

So, strap on your Incredible Shrinking Machine and let's go for a ride.

Start Your Engines ...

- ◆ How your car moves from here to there
- ◆ Looking inside the engine and other moving parts
- ◆ How your car stops and turns without incident
- ◆ Creature comforts for your car

How Cars Run

The first and most important step in keeping your car on the road is knowing how it works. How does it start? How does it stop? What keeps it moving? What the heck is a muffler bearing?

Fortunately, this first chapter graphically covers all these topics—and more—*except* for the muffler bearing because there's no such thing. Don't worry, we won't get dirty. We're going to take a virtual tour of your car.

Get Your Motor Runnin'

What happens when you turn the key in your car's ignition? Lots of things. First, electricity from the battery powers a small *motor* called the starter. The starter motor then makes parts inside the *engine* rotate. Fuel and a spark are fed to the engine to produce thousands of small explosions that keep the parts rotating. Everything else in the car simply uses or supports power from these rotating engine parts.

It's amazing. Technology has enhanced how today's cars run, but the principles of automotive technology are about the same as those of more than a century ago. An electric spark ignites fuel (gas and air) in a small chamber, and the resulting explosion pushes the chamber's floor (piston) down. The power rotates a flywheel that eventually rotates four wheels that roll the car down the road. Sure, there's much more to it, but "internal combustion" or controlled explosions inside the car's engine are the basic principle of most automobiles.

Car Lingo

What's the difference between an engine and a motor? Technically, an **engine** is any machine that uses energy to develop mechanical power and a **motor** is a machine that converts electrical energy into mechanical energy. That means a car uses an engine rather than a motor to drive the wheels. However, most people use the terms interchangeably.

The primary difference between modern cars is whether the engine's power is sent to the front two wheels (front-wheel drive) or back two wheels (rear-wheel drive). Most of the parts in both types of cars are otherwise the same.

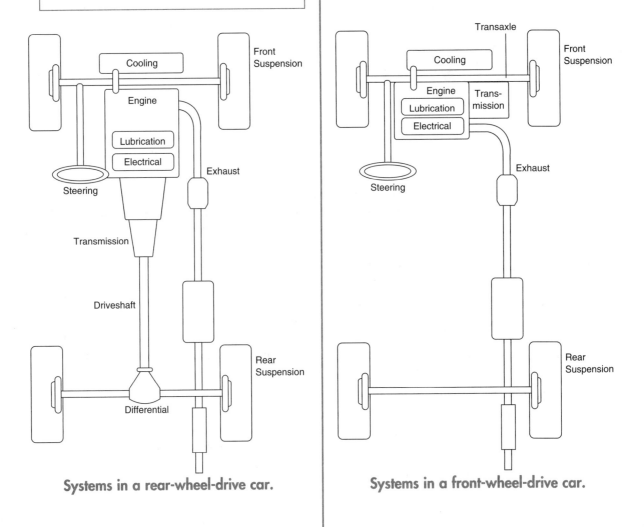

Systems in a rear-wheel-drive car.

Systems in a front-wheel-drive car.

Engine

A piston is simply the movable floor in an engine's combustion chamber. The fuel comes into the chamber through a valve that functions as an automatic door. When the chamber is smallest (the piston has moved up as far as it can go), an electric spark detonates the fuel and causes a controlled explosion. The explosion pushes on all the chamber's walls, but only the bottom wall of the chamber, the piston, can move so it is pushed down. (Just so you know: An exhaust valve opens as the piston comes back up and pushes the burned air out of the cylinder.)

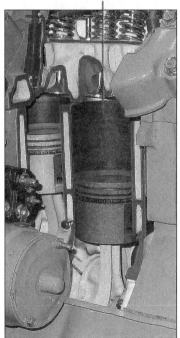

engine chamber (cutaway)

Cross section of an engine's combustion chamber.

How does this explosive power get turned into rotating power? The engine has a *crankshaft* below the pistons. It looks like a straight shaft with bends, called "throws," in it. A connecting rod connects the bottom of the piston to one of the throws in the crankshaft. Downward pressure from the piston rotates the throw in the crankshaft, and thus rotates the crankshaft itself.

 Car Lingo

A **crankshaft** converts the pistons' up-and-down motion into a circular motion that can be used by the transmission and, eventually, the wheels. Bicycle pedals move up and down in the same way to rotate the rear wheel.

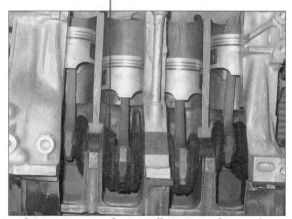

crankshaft

This cutaway of a small engine shows the crankshaft and its throws.

Fortunately, car engines don't have just one cylinder and one crankshaft throw—otherwise the car would lurch down the road with each firing in a cylinder. Cars have four, six, or eight cylinders. That means the crankshaft has four, six, or eight throws connected to the bottom of a piston. By simply timing the explosions and placing the crankshaft throws at angles, the crankshaft's rotation can be controlled so it isn't fighting itself. The crankshaft's rotation turns a round flywheel that turns other parts you'll soon learn about, including the car's wheels.

As you can imagine, there are lots of fast-moving parts in an engine. Pistons, valves, and the crankshaft to name a few. How do they keep from quickly wearing out? Another job of the engine is to deliver oil to parts as needed. *Your* job will be to make sure the engine has enough good-quality oil to do *its* job. (I'll discuss changing the oil in Chapter 7.)

All this combusting makes heat. Lots of heat. So your engine also has a cooling system that removes heat from inside the engine. Therein lies another easy job you'll do: keep the cooling system working well (see Chapters 6 and 10).

The crankshaft's rotation also turns other things on the engine. Belts connect and drive these parts. Some things need to be timed to rotate together, so timing belts are important to an engine. You'll learn lots more about engines, lubrication, cooling, and belts as you discover how to take care of your car.

belts

Belts deliver the engine's power to various accessories.

Starting System

As introduced a moment ago, the starter motor is an important part of your car. It is an electric motor that turns the flywheel that turns the crankshaft that moves the pistons up and down when the car starts. Once the engine is running on its own power, the starter motor *must* get out of the way and quit trying to turn the flywheel. Otherwise the fast-rotating engine will burn up the smaller starter motor. Not good. So an attached electric solenoid engages and disengages the starter as directed by the ignition system and powered by the battery.

Your car depends on an electric storage battery to power the starter motor and dozens of other gadgets. Automotive batteries last a few years without replacement. As you'll learn, simple maintenance can make them last longer.

Some of the engine's power is harnessed to recharge the battery. A contraption called an *alternator* is indirectly connected to the engine's crankshaft using a belt. The crankshaft rotates, turning the belt that turns a wheel on the alternator. The alternator makes electricity that is stored in the battery. You've probably guessed that checking the alternator and belt every once in a while will be part of your maintenance job.

Car Lingo

An **alternator** converts the engine's mechanical energy into electrical power as alternating current (AC). A rectifier then changes AC into direct current (DC) for storage in the battery. A generator, used in older cars, does the same thing in a slightly different way.

alternator

The alternator uses the engine's mechanical power to produce electrical power.

Head Out on the Highway

A twist of the key and your car is running. And *you* know how it works!

Now you have to get the car on the road. You're going to have to feed it some more fuel and get the engine's rotation power to rotate the wheels. Let's see how it's done.

Fuel

Engines live on fuel. In most cases, fuel means a precise mixture of gasoline *and* air. Some vehicles run on diesel (a lower-grade petroleum product) and air.

Part of your car's engine called the *fuel injection system* mixes the appropriate amounts of gas and air and sends it through the intake valve system to the cylinders. Fuel injection systems must be smart. When you push harder on the car's gas pedal it must know exactly how much gas to pull from the tank and how much air it must pull in from outside the engine. It must then mix the two and shoot them into the engine at the exact moment the mixture is needed by the cylinder. There's a valve system involved as well, and the valves, injectors, and even the fuel pump are controlled by a computer—you'll learn about that later, in Chapter 12.

Car Lingo

A **fuel injection system** injects the required amount of fuel at each cylinder for burning. A carburetion system mixes fuel and air for all cylinders in the carburetor and then distributes it to each cylinder through the intake manifold.

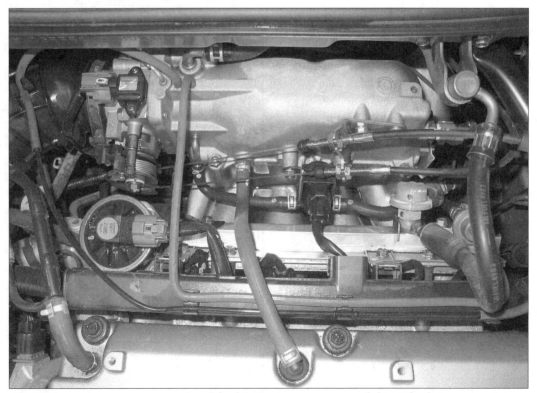

Today's cars use a computerized fuel injection system to deliver fuel to an engine.

Carburetors are no longer used on new cars, but you'll find them on older models.

Fuel injector systems replaced carburetors on most cars about 25 years ago. Carburetors did the same thing—intelligently mixed gas and air. Today's fuel injectors just do it better.

Obviously, you don't want bugs and other contaminants in the air that your engine breathes. Fortunately, cars have air filters through which the air must pass. Changing air filters will be part of your car's regular care, as you'll discover in Chapter 9.

Transmissions

A transmission transmits. That is, it takes the rotation power from the engine's flywheel and sends it on its way toward the wheels. Sure, the engine's rotation could be sent directly to the wheels, but a car's speed would be limited to about 20 miles an hour. That's not practical. So, just like gears on a 10-speed bicycle, the transmission uses the car's momentum to change gears and extend the power available to the wheels.

The first cars didn't have transmissions, so they couldn't go very fast. Today's cars have as many as five gears; first gear is for starting and the last gear is for highway driving. Try starting a car out in fourth or fifth gear and you'll appreciate the function of the transmission.

Technician's Tip

The highest transmission gear for most cars is about 1:1 (one to one), meaning that every revolution of the engine's crankshaft results in a revolution of the driving wheels. Here's the gear ratio for a newer Volkswagen Beetle:

◆ First gear: 3.80:1
◆ Second gear: 2.06:1
◆ Third gear: 1.32:1
◆ Fourth gear: 0.89:1

Changing from one gear to another can be difficult without the clutch. A clutch is a simple device that engages and disengages the transmission from the engine to make the transition between gears smoother.

For many years, all automotive transmissions required some guesswork by the driver. At what speed should the driver change from first to second or third to fourth? The majority of today's cars use an automatic transmission that automatically changes gears as needed. The "clutch" for an automatic transmission is called a torque converter.

gears

This cutaway automatic transmission shows the gears inside.

Differential

The engine's power still hasn't arrived at the wheels. There's one more step. As a car turns, one wheel must rotate faster than the other wheel on the same axle. The differential has small gears in it that distribute the transmission's rotation power to the wheels as needed.

In addition, cars have joints that work just like a knee or elbow. A universal joint lets the drive line between the transmission and differential bend as needed. On front-wheel drive cars the constant-velocity (CV) joint transmits power to the drive wheels while allowing the wheels to be steered and the suspension to respond to bumps in the road. As you can imagine, these joints will need servicing.

You'll also hear the term *drive train* in this and other auto books. The drive train is simply all the components that move the car forward: engine, clutch or torque converter, transmission, joints, and differential or drive axle.

The universal joint is a simple component that transfers power between the transmission and differential while allowing for bumps in the road.

axle   gears

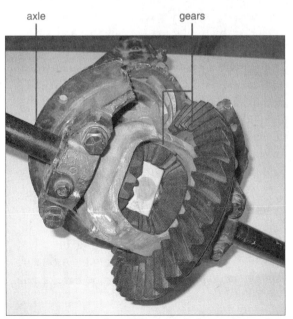

This cutaway of a differential shows how the main gear transfers the transmission's power to the two gears that turn the rear wheels.

CV joint

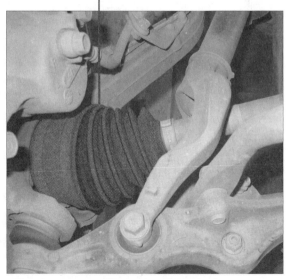

The constant-velocity or CV joint is a more complex version of the universal joint for front-wheel-drive cars. It is housed in a rubber boot for protection.

Lookin' for Adventure

There are many more parts to your car. They all serve a valuable purpose. They help the rubber meet the road. They turn and stop the wheels as needed. They illuminate your car and provide music. And they keep it comfy inside.

Wheels and Tires

We're finally at the wheels. Power generated by the internal combustion engine has traveled through the transmission and differential (together called a transaxle on front-wheel-drive cars) to arrive at the wheels. Wheels are simple. They include tires and rims (onto which the tires are mounted) and the brakes (to be discussed in a moment).

Obviously, tires are important. Tire maintenance is critical to trouble-free travel. I'll show you how to select, inspect, maintain, and even repair tires and wheels in upcoming chapters.

The engine's power is transferred to the wheels and tires to move the car forward.

How "Stock" Is a "Stock Car"?

Ever wonder what's under the hood of that racing stock car that looks a whole lot like yours (except for the big decals)? Jeff Gordon's Chevy racing stock car has a 750+ horsepower engine (a *really* stock Monte Carlo has 200 hp) and requires 108 octane fuel (yours is probably 87 to 92 octane), and it costs about $135,000 (you can buy *five* of the street models for that price). And the tires cost about $400 each and last maybe 100 miles—if the car doesn't spin out at 150 miles an hour! Yes, it's cheaper to drive your look-alike. And you'll get better gas mileage!

Brakes

Now that your car is moving forward, you'll eventually want to make it stop. The brake system does this job. Brake system components include a hydraulic master cylinder and wheel cylinders that transform pressure on the car's brake pedal to move brake parts at each wheel. On disc brakes, small brake pads are forced against a round disc rotating at the end of the axle. On drum brakes, two brake shoes are forced against the inside surface of a brake drum. The friction slows the wheel's rotation and, thus, slows the car.

Obviously, brakes are important. So is brake maintenance. You don't want the cylinders to fail. Nor do you want the brake surfaces to be damaged or wear down too low. Fortunately, this book will show you how to take good care of your brakes so they'll take good care of you.

Here's a look behind a wheel and tire at what a typical drum brake system looks like.

Steering and Suspension

If everyone lived somewhere along a straight road, maybe steering systems wouldn't be needed on cars—until you wanted to turn around. Otherwise, they are a vital part of modern cars. So is the suspension system that makes rides on rough roads smoother.

Components of the steering system include the steering wheel, column, gear, and connections to the wheels so they can turn left or right. The suspension system includes springs and shock absorbers to dampen the effect of bumps in the road.

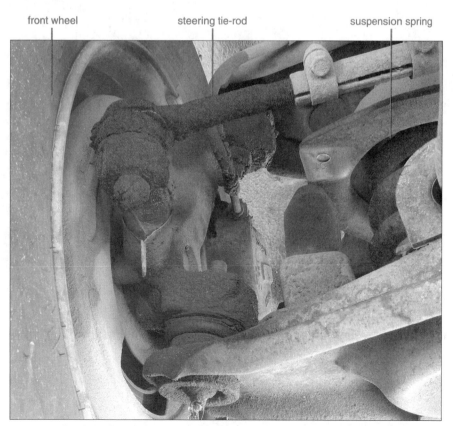

front wheel   steering tie-rod   suspension spring

Here's a look behind the wheel at the steering and suspension system.

Lights

See and be seen. That's the primary function of your car's light system. At night you want to see the road ahead with headlights. When traveling in the dark or when planning to stop or turn your car you want it to be seen with brake and turn lights.

Maintenance is relatively easy: Replace the burned-out bulb. Troubleshooting automotive lighting systems can be more of a challenge. What makes the bulb keep burning out? Or why won't it work after the light has been replaced? What are fuses and how can you replace them? Fortunately, you'll learn how to maintain *and* troubleshoot automotive lighting in this book.

wiring harness   fuse box

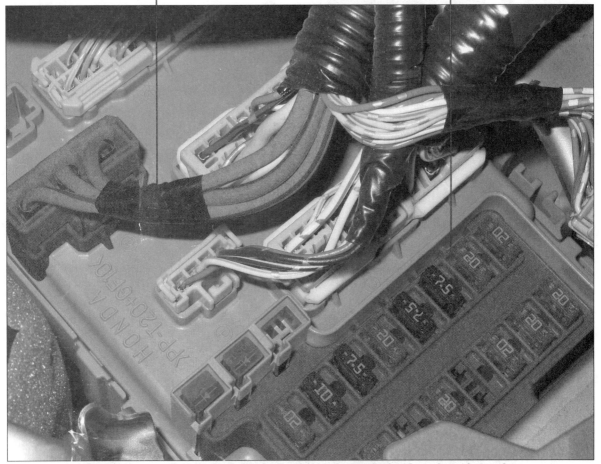

All of the car's electrical system wires run through the fuse box for safety.

In Whatever Comes Our Way

There are still a few more systems in your car. They make traveling more comfortable, entertaining, and informative. Let's take a quick look at each.

Heating and Air Conditioning

Your car's heating system will use excess engine heat to warm the car's interior. The air conditioning system will use excess power (driven by a belt) to cool everyone inside.

Heating and air conditioning systems rely on controls to turn components on and off. Controls may be on-off switches or complex temperature measurements with set points and relays. Fortunately, most are designed to be relatively trouble-free. Unfortunately, they can be a real challenge to troubleshoot and repair. However, learning how they work and staying on top of periodic maintenance can keep them running—and you comfortable—longer.

heater   fan

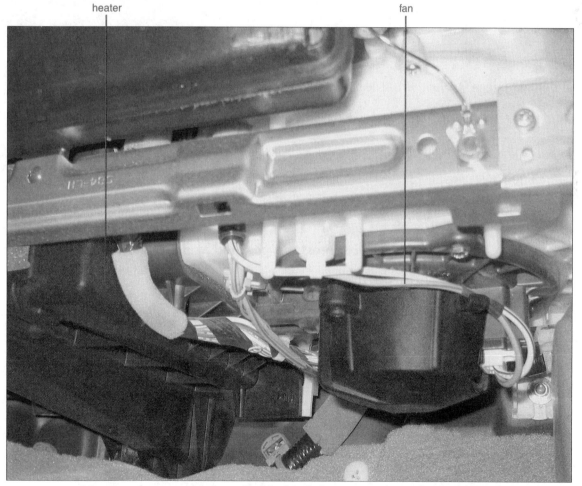

Most car heaters are installed behind the passenger-side dashboard.

air conditioner compressor (mounted on engine)

The air conditioner's compressor is powered by an engine belt.

Sound Systems

Okay, it's not *vital* to getting your car down the road, but the sound system can help make the commute easier. You'd miss it if it didn't work.

Car sound systems can be as simple as a radio in the dash and a couple of speakers in the door—or a six-CD changer with multiple subwoofers that will drain the battery and tax the neighbors' patience. Fortunately, sound systems work on the principle of electricity and can be easily maintained and repaired by the owner. Hey, that's you!

Gauges

With all this automotive technology at your beck and call, it's good to know what's going on. That's where the gauges and controls come in. They continually report how fast you're traveling, how much fuel is in the tank, how well the alternator is recharging the battery, how warm the engine is, and dozens of other important facts. Based on this data you can decide whether to slow down when you see a police car, stop for gas (and a burger) or coolant (and fries), or figure out how far you are from your destination.

Sometimes, however, gauges don't work. That's when your troubleshooting skills will come in handy. If you don't have those skills yet, keep reading. In fact, in this book you'll learn how to read and decipher your car's powerful trouble-analysis system and save you countless hours of head-scratching.

That's how the typical car runs. Next, let's take a closer look at *your* car and see how it's similar, but not the same.

The Finish Line

◆ Cars are powered by an engine that turns fuel into power.

◆ The transmission and differential (or transaxle) transmit the engine's power to the wheels.

◆ Cars have steering and suspension systems to help them turn and make the ride more comfortable.

◆ Other automotive systems support the power system to control climate and entertain passengers.

◆ *You* can maintain and repair your own car!

Start Your Engines ...

◆ Millions of car owners maintain their cars—so can you

◆ Saving money and time at the side of the road with good maintenance

◆ It's relatively easy to learn the specifics of *your* car

◆ How keeping a Car Journal can make maintenance easier

U.S. Owners
Follow the Sever
Maintenance Sch
drive your vehicl
under one or mor
following conditi
• Driving less th
km) per trip or

Knowing *Your* Car

Chapter 1 offered an overview of the *typical* car. But all cars aren't created equal. Some have more valves than others. Some need better gasoline or oil or more frequent maintenance. Some take 4 hours to change a part that can be serviced on another car in 10 minutes.

So this chapter introduces you to *your* car (or cars, or trucks, or SUVs). And it helps you figure out just what it's going to take to care for and repair it. You may decide to do all maintenance and repair yourself—or just the easy stuff. In any case, you'll be able to decide because you *know* your car.

Saving Money with Maintenance

First, let me give a little sales pitch for regular maintenance. Maintenance means changing fluids and replacing worn-out parts as needed. For example, oil that isn't changed when it is full of contaminants can circulate bad stuff throughout your engine. Expensive parts start to wear out and, all of a sudden, deferred maintenance can cause expensive problems. Instead of a simple $20 oil change, you're now paying $2,000 for a new engine. Ouch!

Millions of car owners perform some or all of their car's maintenance—and save money!

Everybody knows that regular maintenance is cost-effective. So why do some cars go a year or more without an oil change that should be done four times a year? Hey, we're busy. We have lives. And we just plain forget.

Good car maintenance is a habit. Just like brushing your teeth, regular car maintenance can save more expensive—and more painful—problems down the road (if you'll pardon the pun). This book will help you make good car maintenance a habit without pulling teeth. It's actually easy to keep your car well maintained.

Technician's Tip

As a full-time auto mechanic and technical advisor for this book, Loren Luedemann says "I don't see many *overly* maintained cars in our shop—mostly ones that are *under* maintained."

Maintenance Schedules

Okay. You're sold on regular maintenance. But what, when, and how? Fortunately, car manufacturers know the answers to these questions and will share them with you. Sure, they want to sell you a new car, but they don't want the reputation of building difficult-to-maintain cars. So they'll tell you how often to change the oil, replace parts, and perform other tasks.

Because all cars aren't created equal, however, the maintenance schedules aren't the same for, say, a Toyota Tercel and a Cadillac Catera. The Toyota folks recommend an oil change every 7,500 miles and the Cadillac people suggest 5,000 miles—under "normal driving conditions."

So what's normal? You would think that "normal driving conditions" means the conditions that most cars face. Wrong. Actually, about two thirds of all cars fall in the *severe driving conditions* category. Lots of stop-and-go driving, driving where the air is full of dust and pollutants, or driving where it gets below freezing or in hot weather more than half the time. That's most cars!

Severe driving conditions typically double the amount of basic maintenance that needs to be done. That means twice as many oil and air filter changes. Fortunately, these aren't expensive maintenance steps, and they can easily be done by most car owners. So you can do a lot toward keeping operating costs down with simple car maintenance.

Car Lingo

Most car manufacturers define **severe driving conditions** as driving less than 5 to 10 miles for most trips, driving in hot (over 90 degree) temperatures, extensive stop-and-go or idling driving (bumper-to-bumper commutes), towing a trailer, or driving in dusty or muddy conditions. If your car is *infrequently* driven under these circumstances, it's considered normal driving conditions.

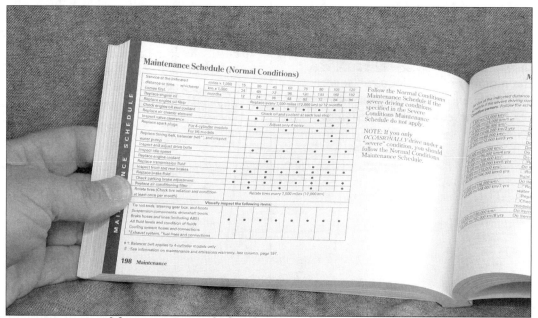

The owner's manual for your car includes the manufacturer's recommendations for service.

U.S. Owners

Follow the Severe Conditions Maintenance Schedule if you drive your vehicle *MAINLY* under one or more of the following conditions:

- Driving less than 5 miles (8 km) per trip or, in freezing temperatures, driving less than 10 miles (16 km) per trip.
- Driving in extremely hot [over 90°F (32°C)] conditions.
- Extensive idling or long periods of stop-and-go driving.
- Trailer towing, driving with a roof top carrier, or driving in mountainous conditions.
- Driving on muddy, dusty, or de-iced roads.

For Canadian Owners

Follow the Maintenance Schedule for Severe Conditions.

∗1 : Balancer belt applies to 4-cylinder models only.

∗2 : Refer to page 240 for replacement information under special driving conditions.

∗3 : Refer to page 239 for replacement information under special driving conditions.

The majority of cars require "severe service maintenance" due to stop-and-go or hot- and cold-weather driving.

Finding Out About *Your* Car

What about *my* car(s), you ask. How often should the oil and filters be changed? What else should I do?

As just mentioned, the manufacturers know this information—and are glad to share it with you. They do so through the owner's manual that comes with new cars, and the shop manuals that consumers and mechanics can buy for specific model cars.

Owner's Manual

If you bought your car new, chances are the salesperson handed you the owner's manual and maybe even marked a few pages with maintenance information. It then went into the glove compartment to sleep. If you bought your car used, you may have an owner's manual sleeping in the glove compartment. There it awaits your discovery.

But what if the manual has vanished or disintegrated? Fortunately, you can buy replacement manuals from the manufacturer, a dealer, or even a used bookstore that specializes in automotive books. To make sure it's the *right* manual, check the car's make, model, and year when ordering. If you have access to the Internet, check out www.bookfinder.com or online auctions such as www.ebay.com.

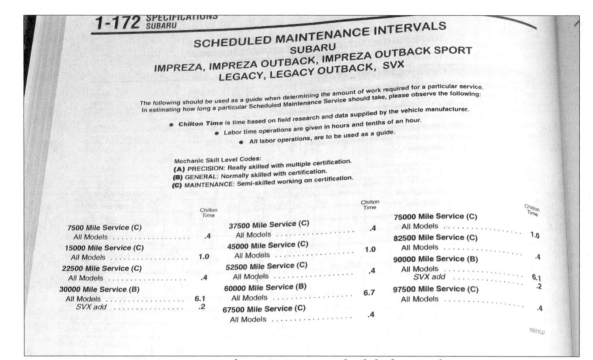

Here's an example maintenance schedule for a Subaru.

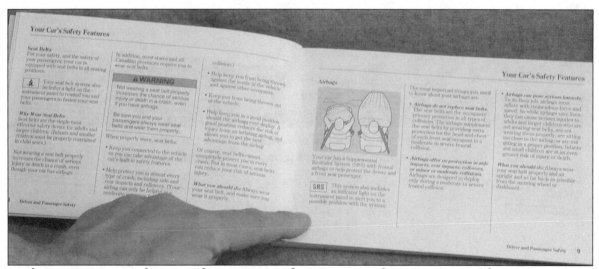

The owner's manual is a vital component of maintenance because it's specific to *your* car.

Shop Manual

The owner's manual concentrates more on operation than on maintenance and repair. For these topics, refer to the shop manual for your car, available through larger bookstores on online.

A shop manual, as the title suggests, is a book you can use in your shop or garage to perform specific maintenance and repair jobs. For example, a shop manual for a Lexus LS400 will have photos or drawings and step-by-step instructions for removing and installing disc brake pads. Also check Part 3 of this book, which includes illustrated instructions for doing the same job on most cars. I'll cover shop manuals in greater depth in Chapter 4.

A general shop manual covers dozens of cars with specific service information not found in the owner's manual.

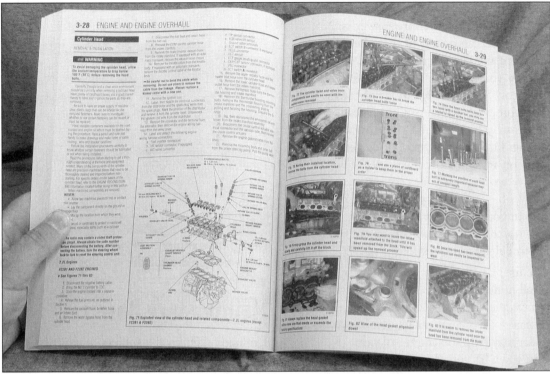

A shop manual published for your specific year, make, and model
of car is the best resource for maintaining and repairing *your* car.

Warranties, Recalls, and Bulletins

Fortunately, new cars typically come with a warranty against defects and abnormal wear for a specific time or number of miles or for various parts. For example, a new car may have a 100,000-mile or 5-year warranty on the drive train. (Remember, that's the engine, transmission and clutch, drive shaft, and differential, transaxle, or rear axle.)

Technician's Tip

The dealer warranty covers squeaks, alignment, and other annoyances for the first 90 days after the sale. The factory warranty covers all parts and systems except normal wear (bumper-to-bumper warranty), the engine, transmission and clutch, drive shaft, and differential or transaxle (drive train or power train warranty), and/or the car's body (rust and corrosion warranty). You can also buy an extended warranty, like an insurance policy, from the dealer on new and used cars. Find out which warranties your car has and if they are still in effect; some transfer with ownership changes and others don't.

Does doing your own maintenance void your car's warranty? The short answer is: No. You, the owner, can do *any* of the scheduled maintenance and even repairs as needed without voiding your car's warranty—provided that you can prove you actually did it right if the question comes up. Of course, the question will come up only if there's a problem with your car and the manufacturer or dealer doesn't want to honor the warranty. Then you'll have to drag out your receipts or logs and show what was done when. By keeping all this info in your owner's manual or in a Car Journal, which I'll discuss in a moment, you'll be able to defend any questions.

Of course, if your dealer notifies you by way of a recall notice that your car has a known manufacturer's defect, let the dealer do the work. It will be paid for by the manufacturer. However, the dealer may try to do additional work at the same time. It's your decision whether to authorize—and pay for—any other work.

How do you know if your car has been recalled? Or what if the manufacturer has sent all dealers a service bulletin (problem report) about your car and they *forgot* to pass it along to you? You can ask the local dealer's service department every once in a while. Or you can check online at www.autopedia.com or www.alldatadiy.com for model-specific service bulletins or even shop manuals.

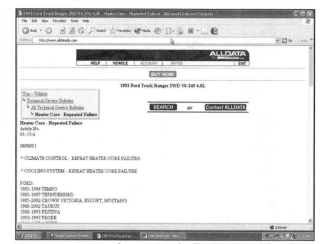

Here's an example service bulletin issued by the manufacturer after the car has left the factory.

Maintenance Basics

I've been skirting the subject of maintenance, warming you up to the idea of doing some or all of it yourself. How much of your car's maintenance and repair *can* you do? The answer is: as much as you want. After reading further, you may decide to do your first oil change, or to perform the annual maintenance needs, or even to replace the car's transmission. Your decision depends on what knowledge, skills, and tools you have. Reading this book will provide the knowledge. Putting it into practice will give you the skills. You'll also learn what tools you need and how to use them. It's up to you.

Many folks who have never performed car maintenance or repairs start with observation jobs such as checking the oil as covered in Chapter 5. They work up to an oil change every three months. Then, if comfortable with it all, they move on to the semiannual and annual maintenance tasks covered in Chapters 8 and 9. Or they tackle some of the jobs and leave others for a trusted service shop or mechanic. They may choose any job that can be done from under the hood, but none that requires jacking up the car or climbing around underneath. Again, it's really up to you.

All you'll need is a schedule (owner's manual), some instructions (this book and maybe a shop manual), some parts and tools (discussed in Chapter 3), and the time. I'll even tell you how much time it should take you to do the job. Men and women of all ages and backgrounds have successfully maintained and repaired their cars for more than 100 years. You can, too!

Repair Basics

Repair is more than fixing problems after they occur—such as replacing a dead engine. Repair is also removing and installing new brake parts *before* they fail. Part 3 of this book covers common easy-to-do repairs with illustrated instructions.

Repairs need the same elements as maintenance: a schedule, some instructions, parts, tools, time, and a place. By performing repairs based on a schedule *you* get to select the time and place it gets done. Even so, you'll soon learn how to tackle needed repairs under adverse conditions.

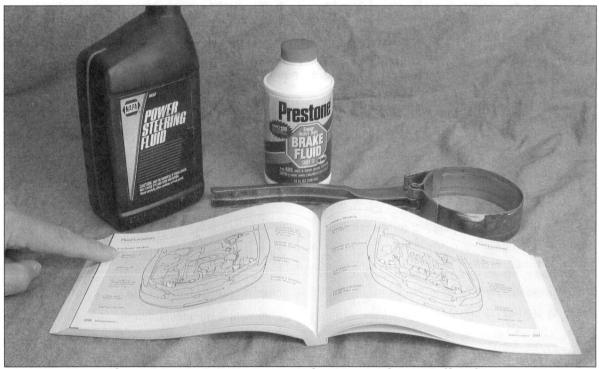

There are many maintenance tasks you can do yourself with just the owner's manual and a few parts and tools.

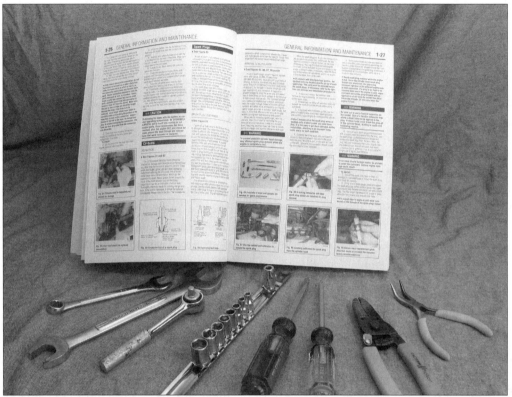

More complex maintenance and most repairs require the car's service manual and basic tools.

Start a Car Journal

You can keep track of your car's maintenance and repairs in the owner's manual. However, you'll soon run out of room for all the information you need. A better idea is to buy a small hard- or spiral-bound notebook for the car's glove compartment and keep track of valuable info. Like what?

◆ Make, model, year, and vehicle identification number (VIN) for your car(s)

◆ Preferred oil brand and weight

◆ Tire size and recommended air pressure

◆ When and where scheduled maintenance was performed, including receipts

◆ When and where unscheduled repairs were done

◆ Part numbers for air filter, oil filter, and fuel filter

◆ Preferred and alternate spark plug part numbers

◆ Recommended spark plug gap

◆ Name, phone number, and shop hours (or business cards) of your favorite mechanics, parts stores, and other service providers

◆ Maintenance checklists

◆ Tune-up specifications

◆ Insurance policy numbers

◆ Miles-per-gallon fuel usage

◆ Reminders, notes, observations, and other important comments

Some car owners use the owner's manual to record anything they want the next owner to see, and their Car Journal for everything else. If you own and maintain more than one car, start a Car Journal for each one and keep it in the glove compartment.

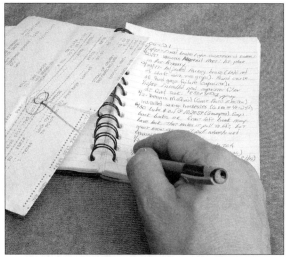

A small notebook can become your Car Journal for recording service as well as parts numbers and other information to make maintenance and repair easier.

STOP **Auto Alert** _____

Make sure your Car Journal has a pocket in which to slip maintenance and repair receipts to prove that required work has been done (a good thing to have if you decide to sell the car). You're not required to use authorized dealers for service to keep the car under warranty. You're only required to make sure regular maintenance gets done—and is documented.

Your Mileage *Will* Vary

As much as modern cars look alike, they are not. Each is an individual with its own idiosyncrasies. Of two cars coming off the assembly line within minutes of each other, one may have more—or fewer—inherent problems than the other. They are designed to be exactly alike, but one may need more maintenance or require repairs earlier due to human foibles.

In addition, how you drive your car can determine its maintenance and repair requirements. The point is that by knowing your car and keeping track of its needs and complaints you can extend its life with little effort. In fact, you might have some fun taking care of your car!

In the next chapter, I'll put some tools in your hands—and show you how to use them.

The Finish Line

◆ Your car has special needs that you can easily learn to help it live longer.

◆ There are manuals written specifically for your car to supplement what you learn in this book.

◆ Knowing what your car's warranties and service bulletins are can save you time and money.

◆ Start a Car Journal to record maintenance, repairs, and to gather receipts.

Start Your Engines ...

- ◆ How to work safely around your car
- ◆ Finding the right parts for the job
- ◆ Gathering the tools your car needs
- ◆ Renting expensive one-time tools to save money

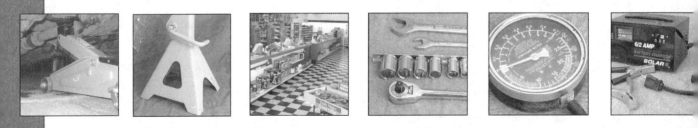

Getting Parts and Tools

In the coming chapters you'll learn how to change your car's oil, check and replace other vital fluids, replace the air filter, and change dozens of worn-out parts. You'll also learn how to troubleshoot and repair just about any problem on your car. For these tasks you'll need parts and tools.

This chapter offers practical tips on finding cost-effective parts and using good-quality tools. Even if you don't own a single tool yet nor have ever visited an auto parts store, you'll find answers here—including the answer to the question "How much of this can I do myself?"

Safe Maintenance and Repair

First, a word to the wise: Do-it-yourself auto maintenance and repair not only save you money (and time at the side of the road); it can also be fun! Those who repair their own cars, or even change the oil, earn bragging rights. They enjoy learning and trying new things.

That is, if they don't get hurt. Unfortunately, engine heat can burn skin, parts can shock or pinch, large objects can fall. You get the picture. Fortunately, millions of folks have worked on their cars with no injuries. So can you. By following some basic principles of safety you can brag not only of your automotive skills, but also of your safety record.

Here are a few common-sense car safety tips:

◆ Cars are designed to roll, so make sure the brakes are set and wheels are blocked so the car doesn't move while you're working on it.

◆ A car jack—a hydraulic or mechanical tool intended to raise a wheel or an axle (with two wheels)—is okay for changing tires, but *not* for safely supporting a car while you're working under it. Before climbing under a car to work, be sure to place sturdy jack stands under the frame so the car won't fall.

A car jack is appropriate for lifting a car, but don't work underneath it until you install jack stands.

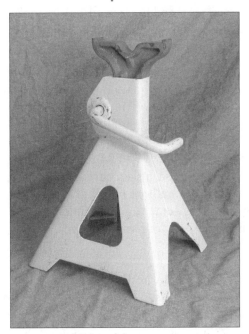

Make sure the jack stands you buy are rated for a load of at least one ton (more is better) and have a full height that will allow you to safely get under the car if necessary.

 Auto Alert _____

A car jack is *not* intended as support for working under the car. Make sure your car has a jack in the trunk (or behind the seat of some pickup trucks). Use stationary locking jack stands to support the car before working underneath it.

◆ Batteries store electricity and chemicals, so be especially careful working around them.

◆ Computers work on very low voltages and are sensitive to excess electricity; nor do they like getting smacked around, so be careful.

◆ Gasoline is a flammable liquid that ignites with a spark, so don't let the two come together except inside the engine.

◆ A running engine has whirring blades, rotating belts, and other moving parts that can catch clothes or skin, so be cautious around it.

◆ The more you know about your car, the safer you will work around it.

Selecting Parts

There are hundreds of makes, models, and versions of modern cars. So how can you find the right part when you need it? Here are some clues:

◆ Until you "know your parts," rely on professional auto parts clerks to help you select the right part instead of heading first for the discount store.

◆ Auto parts clerks are paid to help you find the right part, but only if you give them the right information, so bring along your Car Journal.

◆ If you have a service manual for your car, find the part and any part number in it.

◆ If possible, bring along the part you need to replace so you can show the clerk.

◆ Clean up the old part to see if there are identifiers on it.

◆ Remember that not all parts manufacturers use the same numbering system, so you or the clerk may have to look up equivalent parts in a cross-reference book at the store.

◆ Ask the clerk about the store's return policy on the part *before* you buy it. Most parts stores won't accept electrical parts for return (because they can't test them to see if they still work).

Join a Car Club

Can't find parts for an older car? Consider joining a marquee car club (Chevy, Ford, Honda, etc.), because they often know how and where to get hard-to-find parts. For obsolete (pre-1980s) engine parts contact Egge Parts Company (1-800-866-3443; www.egge.com). For stainless steel replacement fasteners (to dress up your car) contact Totally Stainless (1-800-767-4781). Also, look in used bookstores for interchange manuals that tell you which parts can be interchanged between specific years and models. For example, Ford and Mercury parts are usually similar; Buick, Pontiac, and Oldsmobile parts are, too.

A typical auto parts retailer has extensively more parts, tools, and qualified advice than the auto section of a discount retailer.

Replacing Parts

Parts can be anything from relatively easy to very difficult to replace. In most cases, the problem isn't connecting or installing the part, it's getting to it. Step-by-step illustrated instructions in this book will guide you for many common parts replacements. Beyond that, here are some useful tips:

◆ Many wire connections simply pull apart; if they don't come apart easily, look for a clip or button that can be pushed to release the connection.

wire connections

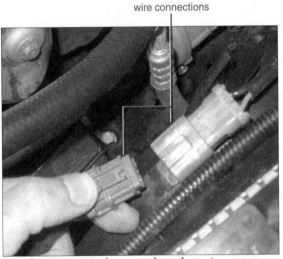

Make sure you know what the wire goes to before unclipping to verify the connection.

◆ Use 1-inch wide masking tape to mark any wires disconnected or extra parts removed so you know how they go back together.

◆ A tight (nonelectric) part that defies removal often can be loosened after a careful spraying with WD-40 or a similar penetrating lubricant product.

◆ If in doubt, ask your auto parts clerk for tips on removing and replacing a specific part.

◆ If you can't find a part on your car, check the owner's manual or service manual for drawings and photographs.

◆ If you find the part that needs replacing but don't feel comfortable tearing things out to get to it, consider letting a professional do it.

Rebuilding Parts

You have choices. The alternator that went bad can be rebuilt or replaced with a new one. Also, you can rebuild yours or you can buy one that is professionally rebuilt. The same goes for an engine that's gone bad—or about to. You can buy a new one, a professionally rebuilt unit, or rebuild it yourself.

Having said that, I'll say this: Don't try rebuilding your own components until you have the experience and tools to do so. Most of these components require specialized tools and knowledge to do the job right. You don't want to trade one bad part for another one.

Technician's Tip

Why consider buying a rebuilt part over a new one? Price! Parts rebuilders can make a part as good as new for less than the cost of a new one. In addition, their equipment and experience means they can rebuild a component better than you can. However, as with all things you buy, make sure you're buying from qualified rebuilders—a trusted auto parts store knows who they are.

In most cases, you don't have someone rebuild your car's part for you, you exchange yours for one that has been rebuilt. So make sure the rebuilt part is an *exact* replacement rebuilt with quality parts and labor. You don't want to try installing a new part that you find out *almost* fits. Nor do you want to save 10 bucks on the part and have to buy a better-quality replacement next month. Many consumers who buy replacement parts do so from rebuilders certified by the original equipment's manufacturer.

Basic Car Tools

With all the automotive tools available today it's amazing how *few* you really need for basic car care and repair. You may even have them in your toolbox right now. If not, here's what you need and why:

◆ Wrenches or sockets to turn nuts and bolts

◆ Screwdrivers to turn screws

◆ Pliers to grab, twist, or hold parts

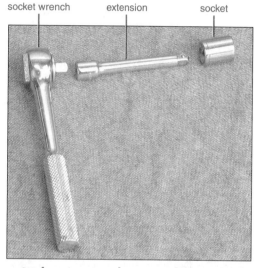

Socket sets can be extended to reach hard-to-get-to bolts.

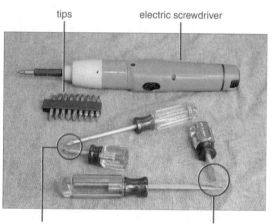

Screwdrivers include manual and powered straight tip and cross (Phillips) tip.

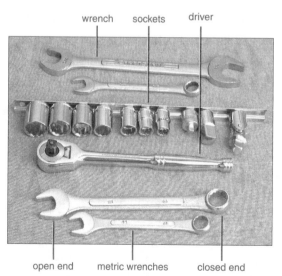

Wrenches and sockets come in all sizes, both standard and metric.

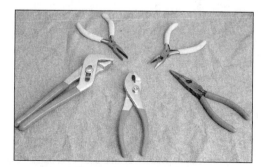

There is a wide variety of pliers that make maintenance easier.

That's about it. You can do a lot with just an adjustable wrench and two screwdrivers (one standard or straight tip and one cross or Phillips tip). So what are all the other tools in a mechanic's tool chest for? To turn nuts, bolts, and screws under special conditions. The bolts may require lots of pressure (torque) to tighten, so there's a torque wrench. To get into some places, larger, smaller, longer, shorter, or more powerful tools are needed. However, the majority of a pro's tools are simply for turning nuts, bolts, and screws.

I'm going to pitch quality again, suggesting that you shouldn't buy tools out of the discount bin at the auto parts or other stores. They typically are made with inferior materials and can break when you need them most. Instead, invest in a good-quality set that will last you many years. A good set on sale costs little more than the junk. And you can pay for the tools with savings from your first (or maybe second) do-it-yourself job.

Another tip: Get what you need. Your auto parts clerk can help you select a tool set that matches your vehicle and your goals. If your car is imported, chances are the parts are measured in *metrics* ("mm" for millimeter) rather than standard ("in." for inches). Don't bother buying a metric tool set for your Buick. However, sometimes it's cheaper to buy a packaged set that includes both standard and metric rather than one or the other.

 Car Lingo

Metric is a measurement system used throughout the world—except in the United States. Parts and tools made elsewhere typically are sized in metrics. Remember: There are 25.4 millimeters (mm) to an inch; ½-inch is 12.7 mm. The most common sizes of metric wrenches are 10, 11, 12, 14, and 15 mm.

For the past 25 years, American car manufacturers have used metric bolts for fastening body parts and some engine brackets and accessories. That means you may find both standard and metric bolts on your American-made car. Make sure the wrench fits the bolt head snugly before using.

And finally, you may need a safety tool or two depending on what you're doing. If you'll be handling a battery or caustic fluids, get a pair of safety gloves. If you'll be working around parts that can fly out, get a pair of safety glasses. Put them in your toolbox—and use them!

Advanced Car Tools

As you progress into the do-it-yourself car care world, you may want to try maintenance and repairs that you hadn't initially considered. You might take a dent out of the body or want to read the car's computer for diagnostics. For these and other jobs, you'll need more than a wrench and some screwdrivers. You'll need specialized tools, such as the following:

◆ Battery charger

◆ Creeper (rolling platform for moving around under a car)

◆ Gear pullers

◆ Hydraulic jack and stationary stands

◆ Engine hoist (for removing an engine)

◆ Electric, hydraulic, or pneumatic power tools

◆ Body maintenance and repair tools

◆ Drills and taps (for making and threading holes)

◆ Vises (for holding parts)

A portable battery charger can recharge an automotive battery in just a few hours.

Creepers offer a flat surface that you can lay on to roll under a car with safety stands.

A hydraulic jack has more lifting power than the scissor jacks included in the trunk of most new cars. (The jack stand is shown earlier in this chapter.)

Buying vs. Renting Tools

Here's a smart option. Instead of buying a shop hoist (for lifting an engine out) or a transmission jack (for lowering the tranny out of the car), consider renting one. You typically can rent a specialized tool from a rental store or larger auto parts store for about 10 percent per day of the actual cost to buy. That is, a $600 hoist (new price) can be rented for around $60 a day. Prices vary greatly, so shop around.

What can you rent? Just about anything. In fact, if you don't plan to do many of your own repairs but need a set of basic automotive tools once in a while, consider renting them. You'll get professional tools at a lower out-of-pocket expense. Expensive automotive tools you can rent cheap include the following:

◆ Jacks to hoist one corner of a car

◆ Jack stands to hold up two corners of a car

◆ Hoists to lift a large component such as an engine

◆ Pullers for removing pressed-on parts

◆ Spreaders for spreading tie rods and ball joints

◆ Separators for assembling bearings

◆ Body and paint equipment

◆ Car dolly or tow bar for moving a non-running car

An engine hoist makes a tough job easy, holding the heavy engine while you carefully install or remove it.

◆ Clutch alignment tool

◆ Compression gauge for testing cylinder compression

◆ Timing light

◆ Vacuum gauge

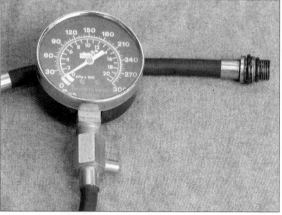

You can rent a compression gauge or, if you have many cars and want to work on all of them, buy one.

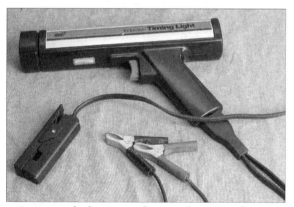

A timing light is used to make sure that a specific engine cylinder is receiving a spark at the optimum moment.

Cars use vacuum power in many ways; you can rent or buy a vacuum gauge to test these systems following your car's service manual.

The Finish Line

◆ Using common-sense safety procedures makes car maintenance easier and less worrisome.

◆ Find a reputable parts supplier that can offer quality advice as well.

◆ Invest in your car's toolbox to save money—and to make the work go easier.

◆ If needed, you can rent nearly any automotive tool rather than buy it.

Start Your Engines ...

- ◆ How and where to find the parts your car needs
- ◆ Figuring out what the maintenance job requires
- ◆ Getting help when you need it
- ◆ Dealing with roadside breakdowns

Finding Resources

You're making progress! You now know how cars work—and you know more about *your* car. You've also discovered how to get parts and tools when you need them.

Fortunately, you have even more resources available to you. Besides making use of parts stores and shop manuals mentioned in previous chapters, you and your car will benefit from having an expert nearby, whether it's a person or an Internet website, or both.

Finding Quality Parts

First, let's take a closer look at finding parts. The temptation for the new do-it-yourselfer is to buy cheap. And it makes sense to shop price if you're buying a new engine or hiring a technician to do the hard jobs. But the difference between the price of name-brand oil at a discount store and that at a quality auto parts store is little; probably less than 50 cents a quart.

Hey, money is money. So why do I recommend that you get your oil from a *real* auto parts store rather than from a discount we-have-everything store? Because you need friends! And 50 cents a quart is cheap for friendship. The big-store clerk, if you can find him or her, may be able to help you find the oil—or not—but probably can't offer any valuable help on selecting it or other parts. On the other hand, the typical auto parts clerk has experience or at least some training in what is sold. They're also easier to find. Don't be shy. Say the magic words, "Can you help me, please?" and you will be amazed at how much value you can get for 50 cents a quart.

Where to start in your quest for a dependable auto parts resource? If your car is less than about five years old, consider starting at the local car dealer's parts department. Buy some oil and a filter and ask for some advice for your first oil change. Because you're looking for dependable help as much as a product, the way the parts clerk treats you is important.

For older cars or if you're not near a dealer, try some of the larger auto parts chains in your area. A quart of oil purchased at each one will tell you lots about whom you should trust for future purchases.

Remember to write down preferred and to-be-avoided stores and clerks in your Car Journal for future reference. Also scribble down any useful advice offered.

Larger auto parts retailers have shelves of service manuals written for the do-it-yourselfer.

Selecting a Technician

As you become more comfortable with doing your own maintenance and repairs on your car, you won't need much advice other than what you can get from your parts clerk. Until then, you may want to find a *technician* to tackle the bigger jobs if needed.

Car Lingo

Yesterday's cars were mostly mechanical; today's are more electrical and computer. So it makes sense that professionals who work on modern cars are now called technicians rather than mechanics. A **technician** is skilled in the techniques (or methods) of repairing automobiles. In fact, technicians specialize with training in one or all automotive systems (engine, transmission, suspension, electrical, and so on).

Like finding a helpful parts store, finding a qualified and helpful technician—at a fair price—is hit-and-miss. For newer cars, start by getting an oil change or other minor service at your local new car dealership. Or ask your friends or your new parts-store friend for recommendations. Look especially for certifications such as Master Technician from the National Institute for Automotive Service Excellence (ASE). You want a trained, experienced technician, not a wannabe.

Your automotive advisor can help you in many ways. He or she can offer instructions or let you assist in a repair—if the shop's insurance policy allows it. Or the technician can tackle the maintenance and repairs you're not comfortable with. Don't expect a reduced price if you assist; consider it the cost of education.

Whether you hire a garage to do the work or advise you while you do it, make sure it has a reputation for honesty, and the technicians have advanced training.

The National Institute for Automotive Service Excellence (ASE) and other trade groups offer courses and certifying tests for automotive technicians and parts clerks.

Reading the Manual

It's good to have a backup technician in case things go wrong or tasks are beyond your comfort zone, but you probably can tackle most maintenance and repair procedures by the book. That book is your car's service manual.

Professional service manuals line the walls at most auto repair shops, offering specific instructions on all cars made in the past 20 years or more. These are the Professional Technician's Editions and include information well beyond what most consumers need or want. For example, it may have a diagram and procedures for securing the rear balancer shaft on a specific engine. You probably don't need this level of detail, but it's good to know that it's available. The cost for a new edition is about $75.00. Used copies for older cars are less than half that amount.

Professional technician service manuals assume technical knowledge and can be difficult to read. They're heavy, too.

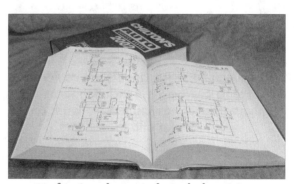

Professional manuals include wiring diagrams like this one, as well as labor time estimates.

For most car owners who want to do their own maintenance and repairs, there are consumer service manuals. Yes, some pro technicians use them, too. But they are really published for the nonprofessional. They include basic information on tools, safety, and routine maintenance for a few model years of a specific make and model. An example is the *Honda Accord/Prelude 1996–2000 Repair Manual* published by Chilton (www.chiltononline.com). It has many more photographs, charts, and diagrams than the pro-level version. It also includes more cautions and safety information than the pro version. The cost for a new edition is about $25.00; less for used editions.

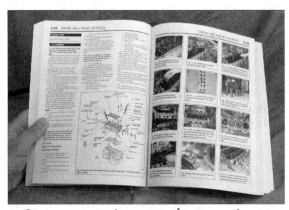

Consumer service manuals are easier to read and typically include more photographs showing how to work on specific make and model cars.

Consumer service manuals also typically include easy-to-follow troubleshooting guides on specific cars.

There's one other book you may want to look at. However, the cost is high and you won't refer to it often, so try to find one in a library or ask your technician or parts supplier to see it. It's called the flat rate book. It includes estimated time for performing most maintenance and repair jobs, by make and model. For example, it will tell you that it will take a trained technician 6.7 hours to perform the 60,000-mile service on a 2000 Subaru Legacy. Because you're not an experience technician, double the time if you have the needed tools. A flat rate manual is handy for figuring whether you have the time (and talent) to tackle a specific repair on your car.

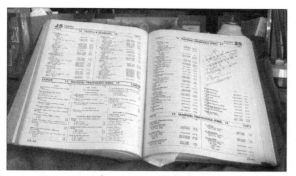

Automotive shops use a flat rate manual to help them estimate the time required to perform a specific repair.

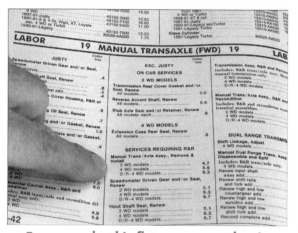

For example, this flat rate manual estimates the time needed to remove and replace (R&R) a specific model car's manual transmission. The mechanic typically multiplies the estimate by the shop's hourly rate to arrive at the total labor costs.

Online Help

It's amazing how much car care and repair help you can find on the Internet. There are literally thousands of websites. If you're not already online, ask a Internet-savvy friend to help you try it out. Or visit a larger library—and plan to wait in line to use a computer. Hey, there are even web cafes where you can rent time on a computer while you sip a cappuccino.

What's the big deal? The Internet is a network that lets computers talk with each other over telephone lines. They share information and even images using a language called HTML for **h**ypertext **m**arkup **l**anguage. As your computer's browser software connects to the Internet, it will read and display HTML files.

For example, all major car manufacturers, most parts resellers, and many parts manufacturers have world websites. Connecting to them, you can find out about the latest models, find a factory-authorized dealer, find parts resources, and more. You can even get questions answered by experts such as Click and Clack, the Tappet Brothers of radio fame (www.cartalk.cars.com). Following are the web addresses of just a few popular online automotive resources.

Two others you may find helpful are www.ownersite.com, which features a vehicle maintenance reminder and expense tracking system; and www.carcarecouncil.org, which includes consumer-level car care advice.

◆ **www.alldatadiy.com**
Automotive data for the
consumer and enthusiast

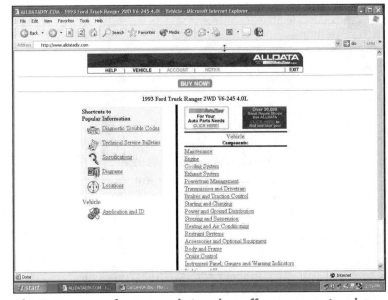

This is just one of many websites that offers automotive data.

◆ **www.autopedia.com**
Automotive encyclopedia
and resources including
links to more than 1,000
auto manufacturer Internet
sites

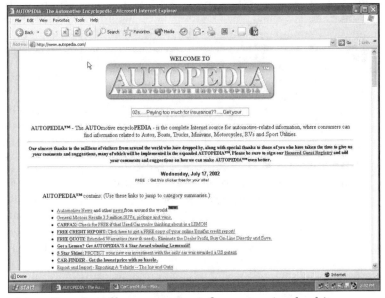

This online site offers extensive information (and ads) on cars.

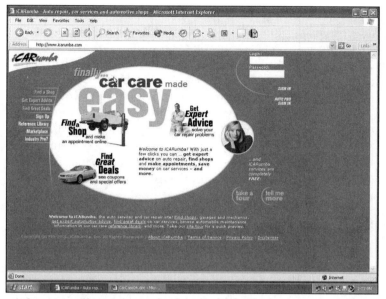

This site offers consumer-level auto information and tips.

◆ **www.icarumba.com**
Excellent online car care
resource

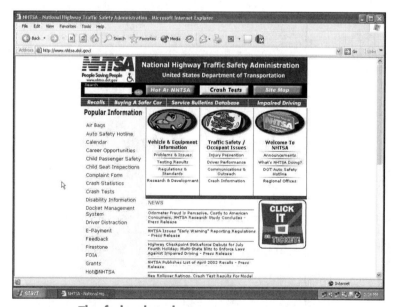

The federal and state governments, too,
have useful websites for car owners.

◆ **www.nhtsa.dot.gov**   U.S.
Dept. of Transportation's
National Highway Traffic
Safety Administration,
source for standards, statis-
tics, and safety information

Setting Up Your "Shop"

If you're going to be maintaining and repairing your car, you'll need some work space. Don't worry, you won't have to buy a new house with a three-bay garage. You can clear out a spot in your current garage or, if you don't have one, rent or borrow a garage. Your "garage" can be anywhere you can tote your tools.

A small portable toolbox can hold the basic tools you need.

A larger rolling toolbox can hold basic and specialized tools for most maintenance and repair jobs you'll encounter.

How much work space do you really need to work on your car? Of course, the answer depends on what you plan to do. As you read Part 2, you'll be inspired to tackle—or to avoid—various car and repair jobs. Most maintenance jobs can be done wherever you park your car. I'll even show you how to change the car's oil without climbing underneath or even getting dirty. So your so-called garage may be a spot in the driveway and your toolbox is stored in the corner of the car's trunk compartment.

However, if you do have some room in your garage, a small table or even a workbench will be handy for laying out parts and tools. You'll want to use a garage if you're servicing or repairing when it's cold or wet outside.

As you become more comfortable servicing and repairing your car, you will want to dedicate a space for the job. Tasks become easier if all tools, parts, and reference books are collected in one place for use. You can start a job and leave it if needed without having to pick up everything and try to remember what goes where later.

Your "shop" can be anywhere you take your portable toolbox (my first shop) to half the garage (my current shop). The best tip is to start small and expand as your needs dictate.

Time to Pull Over

At some time or another, your automotive work space may be at the side of the road. As you do more of your own maintenance and repairs, you'll have fewer breakdowns—and you'll have a better idea of how to fix things. In the meantime, expect an "event."

What can happen?

◆ The battery is too weak to start the engine
◆ A tire is punctured and leaks out all its air
◆ The car runs out of gas
◆ Odd sounds or smells emanate from the car
◆ The engine overheats
◆ Something falls off the car
◆ Someone else's car has a problem and you decide to be a Roadside Samaritan

Knowing this, you can make sure that your roadside shop (that is, the trunk of your car) includes some emergency tools and parts. Here's a suggested list:

◆ The car's owner's manual for instructions on handling specific roadside emergencies, such as changing a flat tire

◆ Safety equipment (flares, reflectors, signs) for signaling traffic that you need assistance or that you need space to work on your car safely

◆ Any cards or telephone numbers you may need for emergency road service (check your auto insurance policy, as many have this benefit included)

◆ Basic hand tools such as wrenches, screwdrivers, and pliers

◆ Any additional tools that will help you in an emergency, such as battery jumper cables

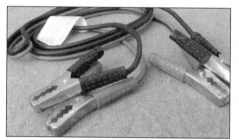

A pair of battery jumper cables is a handy tool for the trunk of your car. Read the instructions in your car's service manual for specifics on how to safely use them.

◆ Extra radiator cap, bottled water in case the engine overheats, coolant, oil, a sealed gas container, drive belt(s), tire sealer

◆ Shop towels (for removing a hot radiator cap and for cleaning up) and hand cleaner

◆ Emergency road service cards and telephone numbers (available through national auto clubs such as AAA and most auto insurance companies)

◆ Anything else that your fertile mind considers for a potential emergency: extra cash, cell phone, first aid kit, warm clothing, work clothes, extra parts that may fail

 Auto Alert _____

"Pull over!" It's more than a police officer's directive. It's good advice. If you're having car problems, drive your car to the side of the road where it will not impede traffic. If the car is disabled, get out on the side *away* from traffic and move away from the car in case it is hit. *Do not* attempt to get out of the car or change a tire when it will put you in the traffic lane. Watch a few episodes of TV's police video shows and you'll see what can happen along the side of a road.

Remember Ramsey's Rule of the Road: Being ready for a roadside emergency reduces the chances of it happening. (But if it *does* happen, you'll be prepared to deal with it.)

The Finish Line

◆ Parts is parts—not! Spend a little more for quality parts and save yourself loads of grief.

◆ An experienced parts store clerk can help you through problems you encounter.

◆ There are scads of printed and online resources available to help you get the job done.

◆ A well-organized shop can cut the time needed to do a job in half.

◆ Be prepared for roadside breakdowns by carrying emergency tools and parts in your trunk.

In This Part

Part **2**

Illustrated Maintenance

That was fun! And there's even more fun coming up. In this part you'll see step-by-step instructions on how to maintain your car, accompanied by lots of photos to show you what's what. You'll discover how easy it is to change the oil and filter, and how to perform many other basic service procedures.

If you'd rather not, the first chapter in this part will show you how to do a simple weekly maintenance at the gas pumps that can save you from being stranded at the side of the road—or in the clutches of Dishonest John's Auto Shop. And you won't even have to get your hands dirty.

If you're hesitant to step into the world of auto maintenance, you're not alone. But fear not! My mechanic and I will be with you every step of the way—and we brought our digital camera to show you what everything looks like.

Let the fun begin!

Start Your Engines ...

- ◆ Easy maintenance you can do at the gas pump
- ◆ Checking the tire pressure and the wheels
- ◆ Looking for problems under the hood
- ◆ Calculating your car's gas mileage

Chapter 5

Maintenance at the Gas Pump

How can you start the habit of car care without planning your life around it? The best place to start is at the gas pump! You have to buy gas, right? And you have to stand there while the tank fills up, right? So why not make those few minutes productive and go through some easy-to-remember steps that can make a difference between an expensive repair and a drive-forever car?

It really can be that easy to start your car care habit. In fact, that's what this chapter is all about. Maybe you'll decide to hire someone else to change the car's oil and tackle other tasks, but if you can get into the habit of checking it every time you fill up with gas, your car can live longer—and make your life a little easier.

Who knows? Maybe you'll spot a frayed belt or coolant drip and get it fixed *before* it strands you at the side of the road.

Pulling Up to the Pump

You can pump your own fuel in nearly all states. And in a couple of states where you can't pump your own fuel, you can get out of the car and perform simple car care tasks without getting arrested.

Before you step out of your car, pull on the hood release handle. It's probably on or near the floor on the left side of the driver. You'll later unlatch the hood as part of your quick inspection.

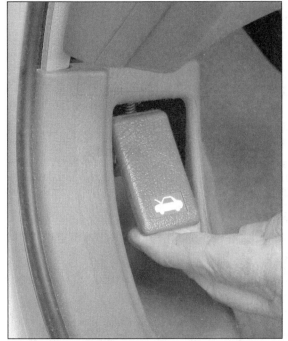

The first step to opening a car's hood is pulling on the hood release handle, either on the left or right side of the driver's seat depending on the model.

If you've stopped to put gas in the car, the first task is to make sure that you're getting the correct fuel for your car. The car's owner's manual (probably in the car's glove compartment) will tell you what quality of gasoline the engine is designed to use; for example, "unleaded gasoline, pump *octane* number 86 or higher." That means the gasoline pump will have a yellow sticker with "86" on it. You can use higher octane fuel, such as 89 or 92 octane, but you won't be getting any benefits from the extra cost. Using fuel with a lower-than-recommended octane rating can cause the engine to misfire and overheat.

 Car Lingo

Octane number is a measurement indicating the tendency of gasoline to detonate (combust at the correct moment) or knock (combust before or after it should). Diesel engines use a cetane number or rating. An engine's designer selects the required octane or cetane number based on the engine's compression ratio.

Make sure you're buying the octane of gasoline recommended by your car's manufacturer. If in doubt, check the owner's manual or call an authorized dealer.

The owner's manual also notes the fuel tank capacity. You can make sure the fuel gauge is working by guesstimating how much fuel it will take to fill your tank. For example, a 17.2-US-gallon tank that's on the one-quarter mark will take about 12 gallons to fill. (Empty isn't really empty; it still has 1 or 2 gallons of fuel in most cars.) So if your car takes significantly more or less fuel to fill than you guesstimated, the fuel gauge may not be functioning accurately.

Checking Tires and Wheels

Once fueling begins, walk slowly toward the front of the car, looking at the tires. I recommend that you buy a tire pressure gauge, or periodically visit a tire store because most of these stores will check tire pressure for you at no charge. Once you've done that, you'll know what the tires should look like. Unless you're having problems with your tires, a quick look at each tire for inflation every time you fill up is all you'll need. Look over the tires for damage as well.

Take a tip from truck drivers who typically check their tires every time they fuel up. As they walk around their rigs they strike the tread of each tire once or twice with a tire iron or wrench and listen. Experience quickly teaches them—as it will teach you—what a properly inflated tire sounds like.

Driving can be cramping to the body, so consider taking an extra moment to squat down and look under the wheels for anything hanging or leaking. The exercise can be good for you—and your car.

Visually check the tires for damage and proper inflation. If you wish, you can also remove the stem cap and use a tire gauge to check air pressure. Once you've done this a few times, you'll know what properly inflated tires look like.

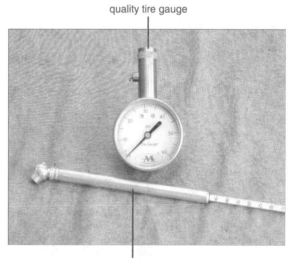

quality tire gauge

basic tire gauge

Two types of air pressure gauges are the dial and the stick. The dial is more accurate—and more expensive.

Under the Hood

You previously pulled the hood release handle inside your car before stepping out. Now you're at the front (or rear, in some cases) of the car and can unlatch the *hood* for a quick inspection of the engine compartment. If you've never tried this before, the latch is a lever under the center of the hood that you push or pull. Its job is to make sure that your car's hood doesn't pop open while you're driving—not fun!

Some car hoods have hydraulic cylinders or large springs at the back corners to hold the hood up while you're peering inside. Many have a support rod that will hold the hood in place. The rod will be lying down somewhere around the perimeter of the engine compartment. One end will be attached to the car and the other can be lifted and inserted in a specially designed hole in the hood's edge. If you're not sure where the rod is located on your car, check the owner's manual.

Car Lingo _____

What's in a name? In the United States, the engine compartment cover is called a **hood.** In Britain it's called a bonnet. Two countries, separated by a common language!

hood latch

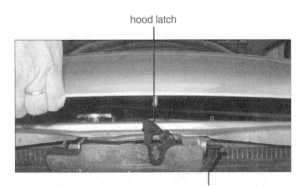

hood lever

Once the hood latch has been released from inside the car, you can unlatch it under the front of the hood.

hood support

Some hoods are held open with springs at the rear of the hood hinge. Others (shown) require a support rod that lies flat across the front or driver side of the engine compartment when the hood is closed.

Opening the hood on some cars is intimidating with all these unknown parts wedged together. Take heart; you'll soon master them!

Now what? There are a number of quick visual checks you can make. Once you've learned more about your car, you'll know where things are and specifically what problems to look for. For example, you may notice that the battery looks gunky, suggesting that the terminals should be cleaned so it doesn't lose power. Or you see that there's a lot of oil sitting on top of the engine, a sign that the oil cap is not on tight.

You'll also visually check the fluids. Many modern cars have a coolant overflow tank near the radiator, and some of these tanks have a "full" mark on the side. (Coolant is a mixture of water and ethylene glycol or propylene glycol in a car's radiator that helps transfer the engine's heat to the air.) If it's low, plan to refill it once you get home where you have tools and supplies (coming up in Chapter 6).

engine

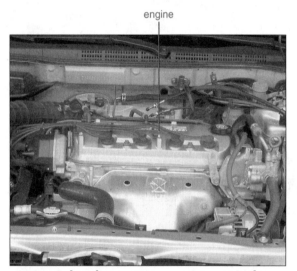

Central in the engine compartment is the engine itself.

battery

At one side or the other of the engine are supporting systems such as the battery, fuse box, and air filter. Your car probably will vary from the model shown here (my 1999 Honda Accord with 60,000 miles), but all modern cars have about the same components.

max   coolant reservoir

min

You can check the coolant level on most cars visually by looking at the side of the coolant reservoir attached to the radiator. If your car doesn't have a coolant reservoir, wait until the engine and radiator are cold before removing the radiator cap and checking coolant level.

You can quickly check the level and condition of the engine oil. Find the oil dipstick and pull it toward you. (If you're not sure where it is, check your car's owner's manual or ask a technician or experienced car owner to point it out.) Check the oil level. It should be at or slightly below the "full" line on the end of the stick. Also check the color and condition. Brown is good. Black is not so good. Water in the oil indicates a leak within the engine. We all know that oil and water don't mix, so the two liquids together on the dipstick will be evident.

Technician's Tip

Not all oil dipsticks say "full" and "add." Some abbreviate levels as F and A or just have two dots with the one closer to the stick handle as the "full" mark. On most cars, the "add" mark indicates that the oil level is one quart low. Check your car's owner's manual for specifics.

Also inspect the windshield wiper tank to make sure it has fluid. You don't need to refill it now, but make a mental note to fill it when you get home.

As you learn more about your car, you will make more extensive visual checks under its hood. You can make sure battery terminals are tight, make sure spark plug wires are securely connected to the plugs, and perform other checks.

oil filler cap   oil dipstick

To check oil, first find and pull up on the oil stick.

dipstick tip

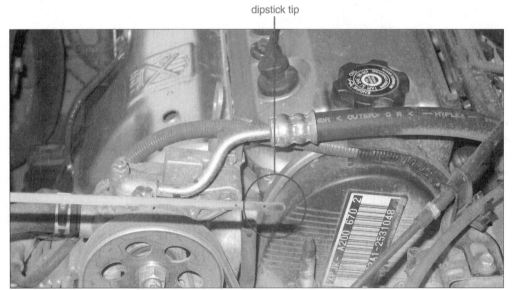

Next, check the reading with the tip lower than the handle.

The windshield washer reservoir on most cars is easy to find and marked with a windshield wiper icon. The dipstick tells you how full the reservoir is.

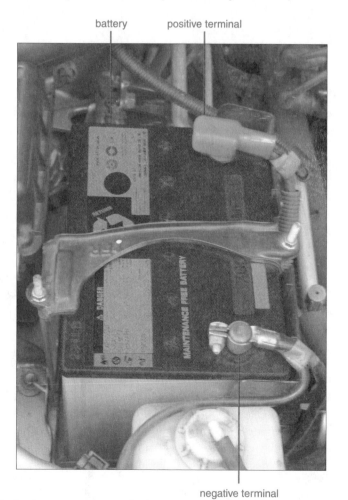

Check the battery terminals for corrosion for a white or gray powder. Carefully wiggle the terminal connections to see if they may be loose.

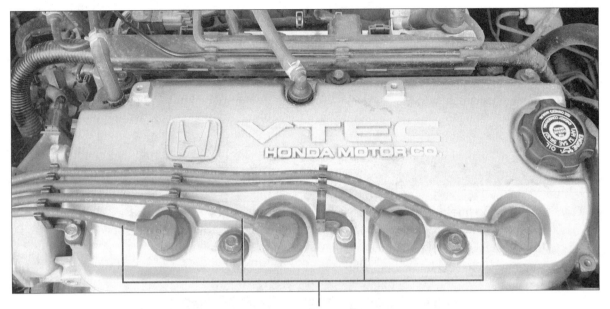

spark plug wires

Inspect the spark plug wires (four for a four-cylinder car, etc.) to see if the insulation seems damaged or the ends aren't connected. The more you learn about your car, the more you'll know what to expect and what to do if you see loose wires.

Follow the spark plug wires to the distributor, where they originate, looking for loose connections or damage.

Most vehicles look about the same when you take their clothes (bodies) off. Many early SUVs, for example, were built on frames and running gear (engine, transmission, differential) used for pickup trucks. RVs, too, are built on truck chassis.

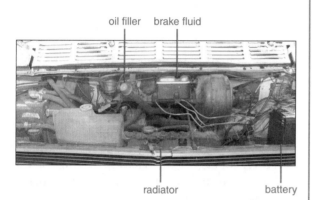

Here's what you'll see if you open the shorter hood on a typical van. Components in a van are in different places than they are in a standard car, but they're all there.

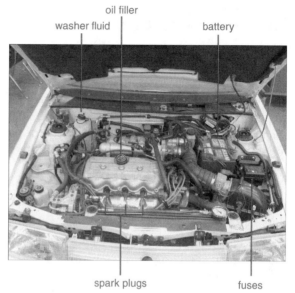

Or maybe your car's engine compartment looks like this one. In any case, in a few minutes you can find the battery, fluid reservoirs—and maybe even the engine in there somewhere.

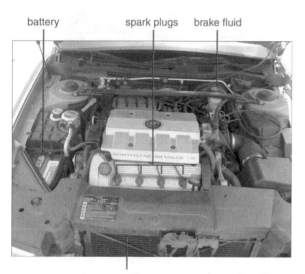

And here's the engine compartment for a newer Cadillac.

Once the hood is closed, continue your stroll around the car and check windshield wipers for damage or loose parts.

Checking Mileage

Once you're done inspecting under the hood, continue your walk around the car looking at tires and wheels until you arrive back at the pump. Once the gas pump shuts off, carefully replace the hose, pay for the fuel, and get a receipt. Your fuel receipt should show you not only the total cost, but also the price per gallon and, very important, the number of gallons of fuel required to fill it. Or, put another way, the number of gallons of fuel used since you last filled the tank.

In the future, you will zero your car's trip odometer so you know how many miles were driven on this tank of gas. All cars have a total mileage odometer below the speedometer. Many have a trip odometer that you can push or twist to return it to zero. Otherwise, you can write the mileage at fill on each of your receipts and do the math later.

Math, you ask? What math? The final step in your gas station maintenance procedure will be to calculate the car's mpg, or miles per gallon. Simply divide the miles driven by the gallons used. For example, let's say the trip odometer (or notation on your receipt) shows that your car traveled 280 miles since the last fill up, and it took 14 gallons to fill it this time. Divide 280 by 14 and you get 20 miles per gallon. (Of course, if other cars are waiting for their turn at the pumps you can defer the math until you get home.)

Take a moment to calculate your car's miles per gallon in your Car Journal.

Auto Alert _____

Did your mpg suddenly drop? The fuel filter may be clogged and need replacement. Or maybe a neighborhood teenager is siphoning gas at night—get a locking gas cap. Also, check the garage floor under the fuel tank for a gas leak. (Look for a stain rather than a wet spot, because gasoline evaporates.)

Why is mpg so important? Other than bragging rights, the mpg figure can tell you how well your car is running. If you write these numbers down in your Car Journal, you'll soon have enough of them to see trends. A gradual or sudden change in mpg can be telling you there are problems with your car. If your driving habits or type of driving (highway, city, country) are about the same, changing mpg can mean the fuel injection or carburetion system isn't working as efficiently. Or it can indicate a deeper problem. The earlier you know that something is amiss, the earlier you can take care of it.

That's about it. Checking out your car as you fill it up can help you identify abnormal conditions before they become problems. And the more times you perform these simple checks, the easier it will become to figure out what's normal and what's not. Even if you decide you _never_ want to change oil or perform other basic maintenance, performing these quick and easy tasks will help you keep your car on the road longer at lower cost.

The Finish Line

◆ Taking a few minutes to check over your car at the gas pump can cut repair costs—and time spent at the side of the road.

◆ Check the tires for damage and proper inflation; take a moment to look at the wheels, too.

◆ Inspect your car's fluid levels to know what it needs to keep you on the road; also take a moment to look for worn parts that could leave you stranded.

◆ Checking gas mileage can tell you how efficiently your car is running.

Start Your Engines ...

- ◆ Checking your car's fluids
- ◆ Taking a look at steering and brakes
- ◆ Checking battery and other connections
- ◆ Keeping your car in good condition

Chapter 6

Maintenance in Your Garage or Driveway

Doing your own simple maintenance checks at the gas pump prepares you for the next step: maintaining your car in your garage or driveway. Even if you've never popped the hood on a car you now can make a habit of car care with just a few minutes.

This chapter offers easy care steps that you can tackle about once a month to keep your car on the road longer. They're basic but important tasks that will take you just a few minutes.

About the only tool you'll need is a shop rag or old wash cloth to keep your hands clean. If you prefer, you can also wear surgical gloves to ensure that oil and gunk won't get under your nails. All of these checks are done at the front of your car, so pop the hood and let's get started.

Opening the Hood

You learned how to open the hood in Chapter 5. As a refresher, most modern cars have a hood release located near the driver. Once pulled, you can move to the front of the car and reach below the slightly opened hood and push or pull the hood release. Then lift the hood and, if it doesn't stay up by itself, find and place the support rod to support the hood. Some of these maintenance steps are monthly expansions on tasks you performed at the pump.

Following are the various checks that most cars have in common. Your car may vary. I recommend that you make these checks in an easy-to-remember order to cut time and to make sure everything gets checked. You can look at the engine compartment from the front as if it's a clock and start your checks at 12 or 6, or you can always start on the driver's side of the car and work toward the passenger's side. Whatever works for you. What's important is time-saving consistency.

These checks are to make sure that the car's vital fluids (oil, coolant, power steering if used, brake, and transmission) are within recommended operating ranges—not too much and not too little—and that some critical parts are in good condition. You really don't have to get dirty.

Reading the Garage Floor

You can learn a lot about your car by reading the garage floor. For example, a puddle of water is condensation from the air conditioner (that's okay). A yellow or yellowish-green puddle is probably leaking coolant. A reddish puddle is usually automatic transmission fluid. A puddle of black liquid can mean an engine oil leak, a manual transmission leak, or a differential lubricant leak, depending on where under the car it is.

The first step in monthly car maintenance is opening up the hood. For safety, make sure the car's engine has been off for at least two hours to allow it to cool down.

Checking Coolant

The first check many folks make is radiator coolant level. This is easier on some cars than on others. The radiator is located at the front of the engine compartment just behind the hood latch. Newer engines made of aluminum don't need as large a radiator as older engines, so modern radiators are relatively small. Because they are smaller, it's even more important to make sure that the engine has sufficient coolant. An aluminum engine without coolant can destroy itself in minutes.

Notice I didn't say "water," but "coolant"; there is a difference. Coolant for most cars is a mixture of half water and half antifreeze. (The car's owner's manual will be more specific.) In colder climates, coolant may be 75 percent antifreeze.

Many cars have a plastic coolant reserve tank at one side or the other of the radiator. If so, there are probably marks on the side of the tank indicating "full" or "max" and "low" or "min." If the coolant level is between these two lines, add coolant until the level is at the "full" or "max" line. Don't overfill!

If the coolant is below the "low" or "min" line, or your car doesn't have a coolant reserve tank, carefully remove the radiator's cap and *slowly* fill the radiator with coolant. (Filling slowly allows air in the radiator to escape.) Wear protective gloves or use a thick rag to protect your hands. Most radiator caps are turned counterclockwise to remove and clockwise to tighten. Once full, reinstall the radiator cap and, if needed, fill the reserve tank.

STOP **Auto Alert**

Be *very* careful when removing the radiator cap because the hot coolant is under pressure and can scald your skin. Radiator caps can be loosened in steps, turning slightly to release pressure without blowing the cap off. It's safer to take an extra 15 minutes or more and let the radiator cool down before opening the cap.

Finally, wipe up any excess coolant because it can damage some paint finishes. In addition, coolant is toxic, especially to small children and animals.

cloth (to protect paint from coolant)   funnel

reservoir

If the coolant level is low, fill it with the antifreeze-and-water mixture recommended by the manufacturer in the car's owner's manual. Use a funnel to prevent spills.

If the coolant reservoir is empty—or your car doesn't have one—carefully remove the radiator cap and use a funnel to fill the radiator with coolant directly.

This is a good time to check the radiator hose by carefully squeezing it and looking for cracks. If it needs replacement, see Chapter 11 or your favorite mechanic.

Periodically check the condition of your coolant with a coolant test kit available at larger auto parts stores.

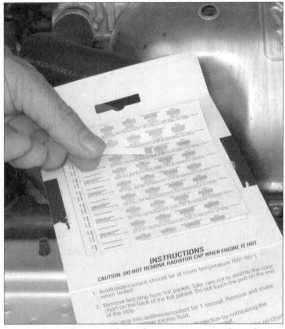

Compare the results of your test to the chart that comes with the test kit to know if the coolant will do its job as is or needs more antifreeze or replacement of antifreeze.

Checking Washer Fluid

Here's another easy one. The windshield washer can spray soapy water on your car's windshield to help keep it clean. The washer gets the fluid from a clearly marked reservoir in the engine compartment. Most are easy to find and to refill.

To refill, remove the reservoir cap and pour windshield washer fluid in the tank until the level is near the top. The fluid is water, some soap, and maybe some alcohol or other chemical to keep the mixture from freezing when it's cold outside. Alternatively, you can use plain water when it's warmer.

To fill the washer fluid reservoir, open the top and pour in windshield washer fluid (available at auto parts and other stores). The fluid contains a mild soap and some alcohol to keep it from freezing during the winter.

Checking Oil Level

Oil is your engine's blood supply. Newer and well-maintained engines don't use up or leak very much oil, so checking oil means testing it for grit and water—two things you don't want running around in your engine. Older engines may burn oil (oil actually gets inside the cylinder and explodes with the gas mixture!) and must be replaced. So you'll also be checking to make sure that the oil level is full.

As mentioned in Chapter 5, start by finding your car's oil measurement device, called a dipstick. It's so called because it is a long, slender, metal stick with its head at the top of the engine and its bottom tip in the oil that coagulates at the bottom of the engine. By pulling the dipstick out of the engine and inspecting the tip, you can see the level of oil in the engine.

Technician's Tip

Remember to keep the dipstick's handle higher than the tip you're reading. Otherwise the oil will run up the stick and give you a false reading.

So it makes sense that you want to make sure your car is relatively level when you check its oil. And the car's engine should be off for a few minutes so that the circulated oil drains down into the bottom of the engine (called the oil pan). Also, make sure the dipstick has been pushed down as far as it will go in its tube so it gives an accurate reading of the depth of the oil in the pan.

It actually takes longer to read about checking oil than to do it. Lift the dipstick from its tube and check where the top edge of the oil is. If you have any doubt, wipe the dipstick clean with a rag and reinsert it all the way into the tube for a moment and withdraw to verify your first reading. (Check the car's owner's manual if you're not sure where the "full" line is.)

The dipstick is easy to find on most modern cars—once you know what to look for. Many are color-coded or have a loop at the end of the dipstick handle.

Next, wipe some of the oil on a bare or gloved finger and rub it between a finger and thumb to feel whether it's gritty. Also, look at the oil to see if it looks like some water is in it. Oil and water don't mix, so the water should be obvious. Finally, hold the end of the dipstick or your oily fingers up to your nose and smell the oil. If it smells burnt it probably is, indicating it's time for an oil change (see Chapter 7).

Rub some of the oil between your fingers to see if it's gritty, a sign that there's wear in the engine and the oil should be changed.

Note that as you perform your car's maintenance on a regular schedule, you won't have to do the look-rub-sniff test to find out how the oil is holding up. You'll be changing it *before* there are oil problems. Even so, periodically inspecting your oil between changes is a good way to read your engine's condition, as you will learn in coming chapters.

Another note: If buying a new-to-you car, the look-rub-sniff test can help you determine if the car's oil has been properly maintained. It's also a good indication of how the car has been cared for overall.

Checking Transmission Fluid Level

Automatic transmissions need fluid, too. To check fluid level, first make sure the car is parked on a level spot (for the same reason as when you check engine oil level). Most cars require that the engine be running and the transmission be in either park (P) or neutral (N) gear. Find the automatic transmission fluid dipstick, pull it out, and wipe it with a clean cloth. Insert the dipstick all the way into the transmission securely, then withdraw it to check the fluid level. It should be between the upper and lower marks. If the fluid level is low, add *automatic transmission fluid* (*ATF*) until the

level reaches the "full" mark. Check your car's owner's manual to see which type is approved by the manufacturer.

Most manual transmissions don't have a handy-dandy dipstick. Instead, they are checked from underneath the car. Fortunately, fluid level doesn't have to be checked often. I'll cover how to replace transmission fluid in Chapter 10.

Car Lingo

Automatic transmission fluid (ATF) is a thin petroleum designed to freely flow through the transmission's hydraulic components. It also contains additives to keep it clean and extend its life.

automatic dipstick   ATF fill

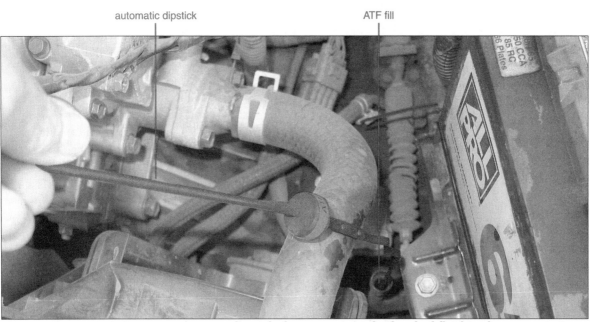

Automatic transmissions, too, have a dipstick that measures the level of fluid in the transmission.

Use a funnel to add automatic transmission fluid, making sure you're using the type required by the car's manufacturer.

Checking Steering and Brake Fluids

Modern cars have other fluids that are nearly as important and just about as easy to check. Steering systems use a special hydraulic fluid that makes steering easier. This is a special thin, lightweight oil that transmits power or force. Brakes use a different type of hydraulic fluid that magnifies your foot's pressure on the brake pedal to make brakes at all four wheels slow your car down.

One to Steer, One to Brake

Steering and brake fluids are *not* interchangeable. In fact, you should only use the exact type of fluid recommended by the manufacturer when replacing fluids (check the owner's manual). For example, brake fluids come in at least three specifications: DOT 3, DOT 4, and DOT 5. (DOT stands for U.S. Department of Transportation.) If your car's manufacturer calls for DOT 3 brake fluid, *do not* use DOT 4 or DOT 5 unless the manufacturer says you can. Why? Because these hydraulic fluids have different additives that work well in one type of brake but can actually destroy another. Also, brake fluid is relatively cheap so don't use it from a can that's been opened more than a year.

Checking steering fluid is relatively easy. Most cars that use steering fluid provide a well-marked tank in the engine compartment somewhere on the driver's side of the car. In fact, many are translucent with a "full" line that can be read without opening the top. Or you can simply twist off the steering fluid cap and use the short dipstick attached to the cap to check the fluid's level. If you're not comfortable with checking or replacing the steering fluid, ask a trusted mechanic or full-service station attendant to do so. I'll expound on brakes and steering in greater detail in Chapter 8.

Brake fluid is also important to your car's well-being. To check brake fluid level, you may need to remove the master brake cylinder's top and visually check it. Many master cylinders have a reservoir similar to the one for the steering system. (Be careful not to get them confused and add the wrong fluid!) Others have a metal cap with a pressure clip that must be carefully pried off with a screwdriver to check the level. Again, if you're not comfortable doing this, hire someone who is and watch how it's done. Or refer to the car's owner's manual or service manual for specific instructions.

As with many other car fluids, power steering fluid (PSF) can easily be checked by reading the side of the reservoir for "max" and "min" or "full" and "low" indicators. To replace fluid, remove the reservoir cap. Use only power steering fluid recommended by the car's manufacturer.

Fill the brake fluid reservoir to the "max" or "full" level.

A set of plastic funnels can be handy for adding liquids to your car's systems. This set costs less than $3 and includes three funnels of various sizes.

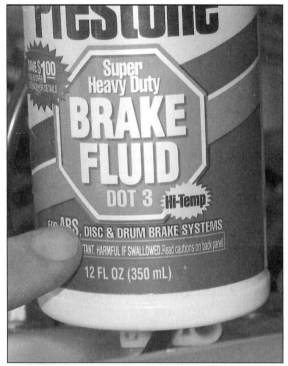

Make sure you use the correct type of brake fluid as recommended by the car's manufacturer. If in doubt, ask your auto parts clerk.

Some cars use a fluid for the manual transmission's clutch system. It, too, is a hydraulic fluid used in a booster that makes depressing the clutch pedal easier. If your car is so equipped, look for a small reservoir clearly marked for "clutch fluid" and remove the cap to look for a fluid level indicator. The cap (or owner's manual) will tell you what fluid to use when refilling.

Cars with manual transmissions may have a hydraulic-assisted clutch that requires clutch fluid if low. Your owner's manual, auto parts retailer, or car dealer can tell you what type to get.

Checking Battery Connections

Once a month, check the connections on your car's battery to make sure they are clean and well connected. If the battery isn't maintenance-free (most are today), you may need to check the fluid level in the battery cells, too. If the fluid level is low, carefully refill with distilled water. Don't overfill, because caustic battery acid can overflow and possibly burn the skin. If spilled, immediately wash the affected area with lots of water. Most modern batteries are sealed so you can't fill them.

This is another job that takes longer to read about than to do. Once familiar with it, you can check battery connections in just a few seconds.

All you're doing is carefully wiggling the battery cables at the two terminals. Because the battery is full of acid and electricity, treat it with the proper respect and don't try touching the terminals without gloves—or at least a clean rag—between you and the battery. If the terminals are loose, carefully tighten them with the proper-size wrench.

If the terminals have a white or light-colored power on them, carefully clean the terminals with a brush or rag, being very cautious as the dust is corrosive (be sure to wear gloves). If you're not comfortable doing this, take your car to a battery shop or a trusted mechanic. If you want to do it yourself, unloosen the terminals and use a battery brush to clean the terminals and posts. Your auto parts store may have a

battery terminal cleaner, or you can carefully apply a solution of baking soda and water. Then apply a battery gel or washers that minimize corrosion.

Auto Alert

Many jobs around your car require that you disconnect the negative terminal on your car's battery for safety. On many cars, doing so may require that you reset a security code. Read the owner's manual for specifics *before* disconnecting the battery. Also, be aware that some car computers will automatically clear diagnostics codes from memory if the battery is disconnected.

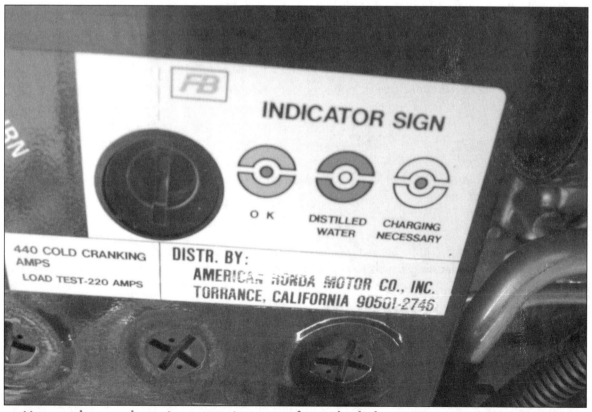

Most modern car batteries are maintenance-free. Check the "eye" on top (see instructions on top of the battery or in the car's owner's manual) to read the battery's condition.

positive terminal   negative terminal

Disconnect the negative and then the positive battery terminal, and clean the posts with a battery post-and-terminal cleaning brush available at your auto parts retailer.

Open the top of the cleaning brush to reveal a special brush for cleaning inside the terminals.

Checking Other Connections

There are dozens of other parts in the engine compartment that can be checked to make sure they are solidly connected. As with other tasks, once you're familiar with things in the compartment it will take just a few seconds to wiggle and make sure everything is well connected.

Here are some suggestions on what connections to check for typical cars:

◆ Spark plug wires
◆ Electric wire connections
◆ Belts

spark plug wires

As you did with your maintenance steps at the gas station, inspect the spark plug wires. This time, look more closely at the wires and connections to make sure they're in good condition.

Inspect the belts that power the alternator, air conditioning compressor, and other components. Refer to your car's service manual for specifics on tightening or replacing the belts.

Lubrication

Finally, take a few minutes to lubricate door hinges and other moving parts on your car. Which ones? Your car's owner's manual will probably list them. Some service manuals have a list, too.

Car lubricants include the ever-popular WD-40, which is also handy for loosening stuck bolts and other fasteners.

Many car owners stop here and hire others to do the work—but they don't have to. It's a choice. Doing it yourself can not only save you money, but also help you understand your car better—and help you prevent future problems.

The Finish Line

◆ You can perform monthly maintenance steps in your driveway or garage in less than an hour.

◆ The most important step to monthly maintenance is making sure that your car's fluids are at the correct levels and adding to them when they're not.

◆ Make sure your car's system connections all share power and information by keeping them clean and tight.

◆ Don't forget to lubricate your car's door hinges and other moving parts.

Start Your Engines ...

- ◆ How oil protects your car's engine
- ◆ Figuring out how often to change your car's oil and filter
- ◆ Gathering tools and parts for an easy oil change
- ◆ How to select the right oil and filter for your car
- ◆ Step-by-step instructions for changing your car' s oil and filter

Changing Oil and Filter

As you've seen, oil is the lifeblood of your car's engine—and the engine is a pretty important part of your car. So making sure that the oil is doing its job is a vital part of maintenance.

Here's where you can save some time, money, and potential repairs with an investment of less than $15 in parts about four times a year. This chapter offers step-by-step instructions for the most popular do-it-yourself car care job: changing oil and filter. It includes info on exactly what parts and tools you'll need to do the job in less than an hour. Once you get some experience, you can cut that time in half. And you'll know the job is done by someone who cares about your car, rather than by a minimum-wage daydreamer who may forget to put on the new filter.

Understanding Oil

The crankshaft makes 1,000 to 6,000 revolutions per minute (rpm). That's a lot of metal-on-metal friction. What keeps the engine from burning up is *oil*. In addition, additives such as cleaners help the oil remove and suspend carbon (from the fuel burning process) and fine metal particles (from wear). Oil is a great lubricant and won't wear out (quit lubricating) for a long time.

As the oil circulates through the engine, it passes through a filter that traps the suspended carbon and metal particles—until the filter becomes saturated. Then the bad stuff circulates with the oil, potentially causing damage to the engine's moving parts. If nothing else, the saturated oil begins clogging the engine's "arteries" or oil passages until the engine finally has a "heart attack" or failure. Think of bad oil as bad cholesterol for the engine.

Car Lingo

Oil is a petroleum product that lubricates metal parts to reduce wear due to friction. Synthetic oil offers the same or better properties, but is more expensive. Blended oil combines petroleum and synthetic oils for some benefits at a lower cost.

engine cylinder
(cutaway)

oil plug   oil pan   oil filter

The engine is constantly being lubricated by the oil system that circulates oil from a pump located in the oil pan through the engine and finally through the oil filter.

In addition, acids build up in oil. As the engine reaches running temperature, some acids are removed by the positive-crankcase ventilation (p.c.v.) valve. Short road trips don't allow the engine to reach optimum temperature, so acids stay in the oil and the oil needs to be changed more often.

How Often?

So when should you change the oil in your car? Obviously, *before* the oil becomes a problem rather than a solution. When is that? Car manufacturers recommend changing oil every 5,000 to 7,500 miles under normal conditions. However, as I mentioned back in Chapter 2, the majority of cars (about two thirds) are driven under severe conditions—cold climates (where oil has to work harder), dusty locations (where sand or dirt particles from the outside air can enter the combustion chamber), or on lots of short or stop-and-go trips (when the engine doesn't warm up or oil doesn't circulate well).

Under these conditions, most car manufacturers suggest that you change the oil twice as often. That means every 2,500 to 3,750 miles—or every three months, whichever comes first. The additives in oil can lose their functionality if they just sit inside the engine for months without being circulated, so a time limit is suggested.

Okay, here's *my* recommendation, based on owning and maintaining numerous cars, trucks, and RVs over nearly 40 years and asking dozens of experts for their advice. *Change the oil and filter in your car every 3,000 to 5,000 miles or every three months, whichever occurs first.* You really don't have to pull over to the side of the road and change the oil at 3,125 miles! You can guesstimate when it will be needed again and schedule it to fall on a day off or when it's most convenient. Just keep this fact in mind: An oil change costs less than $15 in parts—less than 1 percent of the cost of a new engine!

Technician's Tip

If your car is still under new-car warranty, make sure you change the oil at
least as frequently as is recommended by the
manufacturer. Also, keep a record of oil/
filter changes in your Car Journal, and hold
on to receipts to show when and how often
you changed the oil and filter.

Okay, I'll stop talking and show you how to
change your car's oil and filter in a matter of
minutes.

There is a wide variety of oil brands,
blends, and weights available. Your best bet
is to stick with the manufacturer's recommendation as found in the owner's manual.
However, older cars that burn oil may need
a heavier-weight oil (40 instead of 30).

Getting Ready for a Change

The first step in an oil change is gathering the
needed parts and tools in a safe work environment. Here's what you'll need:

- 4 to 5 quarts of oil (see "What Kind of
  Oil?")
- Oil filter (see "Buying an Oil Filter")
- 5-quart (or larger) oil collection container
- Oil funnel
- Drain plug wrench

- Oil filter wrench
- Jack and jack stands for supporting the
  car
- An old blanket or a mechanic's creeper
  for going under the car
- Protective gloves or hand cleaner

The first step to an oil change is gathering the
needed oil, filter, wrenches, and oil collector.

That's about it. In fact, you can buy a year's
worth of oil and filters and store them so you
don't have to run out to buy everything at the
last minute. Oil in a can or bottle can be stored
for two years or more, depending on what additives are in the oil.

You're a good environmental citizen so you're
going to properly dispose of the oil once it's
drained. Fortunately, many auto parts retailers
have facilities for recycling used oil, so find out
when you buy your oil how to best dispose of it.
Alternatively, there are environmentally friendly
oil collection containers that absorb the old oil
so it can be trashed. Your auto parts store can
tell you what's available—and what's allowed.

What Kind of Oil?

Your car's owner's manual will tell you not only how much oil is required to fill it, but also what grade or weight of oil. The weight measures the viscosity or thickness of the oil. Ten-weight oil is thinner than 30-weight oil. Most modern cars use multiviscosity oil, two weights such as 10-30. A 10W-30 oil acts as if it's 10-weight when it's cold (less drag when starting the engine) and 30-weight when it warms up. The W in 10W is the "winter weight." As a car's engine begins to wear, heavier-weight oil can keep it from "burning" oil (actually losing oil around the pistons). One more thing: Buy oil that's rated for gasoline engines—unless your car's engine is diesel. If in doubt, ask your favorite auto parts clerk.

Buying an Oil Filter

Early cars didn't have oil filters. You simply ran your car for a month or 1,000 miles, then drained the oil into a bucket or onto the ground somewhere, replaced the plug, and refilled the oil. Today's cars use an oil filter and better oils with additives to put thousands of miles between more environmentally friendly oil changes. The *right* oil filter for your car is one that meets or exceeds the manufacturer's recommendations. Each brand of oil filter may have a different part number, but all are cross-referenced in a parts book at most auto parts stores. Which brand of filter should you buy? Ask your parts supplier for a recommendation.

Technician's Tip

Because oil filter cartridges are made up of filter paper, the heavier the filter unit, the better quality it probably is.

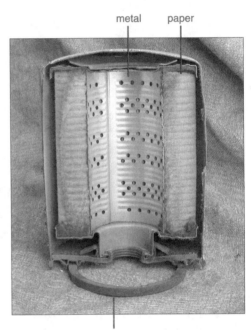

metal   paper

rubber seal

Here's what the inside of a typical oil filter looks like. It's basically a metal can with a paper filter.

Changing Oil and Filter

As an overview of the impending job, you're going to drain all of the oil from the engine into a container and remove the old filter, then replace the filter and oil with new stuff. Here are the steps:

1. Run the engine until it reaches normal operating temperature (so the oil flows easily), then turn the engine off. (Of course, make sure your work space has sufficient ventilation.)

Once run, the engine is hot! Be very careful what and where you touch. If in doubt, hold your hand near the object to feel heat. If you think a part is cool, touch lightly to verify.

2. Remove the oil filler cap located on the top of the engine's valve cover, typically marked "oil."

oil filler cap   oil dipstick

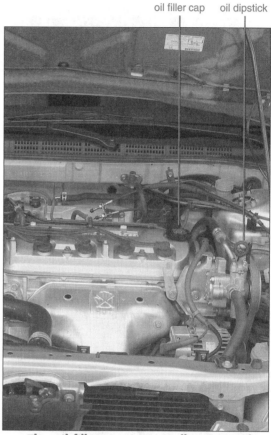

The oil filler cap is typically mounted on top of the engine.

3. Set the emergency brake, then raise and safely support the front (or back) of the vehicle, depending on where the engine is, with a jack and jack stands.

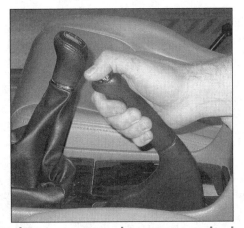

Make sure you set the emergency brake before jacking up the car so it doesn't roll.

You can use your car's tire jack (typically located in the trunk) or a hydraulic floor jack for lifting the car. Because you'll need to go partially under the car to reach the oil pan drain nut, make sure jack stands are installed under the frame.

4. Slide the drain pan under the oil pan's drain plug, a bolt head located at the lowest point on the engine. Be careful to not touch the warm engine.

oil drain plug

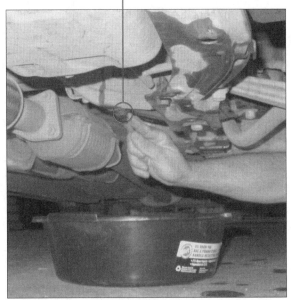

Make sure the oil collection pan is located directly under the middle of the oil drain plug.

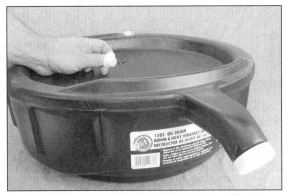

Here's an alternative style of oil collection pan with a lid and a cap that makes it less likely to spill when carried for disposal.

5. Loosen the drain plug using a correctly sized socket or box wrench (*not* an adjustable wrench) so the plug isn't damaged.

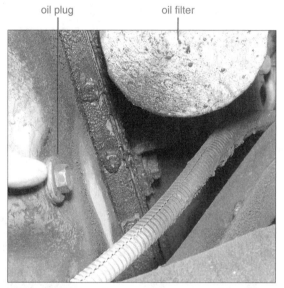

oil plug   oil filter

Make sure you loosen the correct plug. The engine oil plug is located on the lowest point of the engine, on the oil pan. Some transmissions have drain plugs as well; however, the transmission is behind the engine (rear-wheel-drive cars) or to one side of the engine (front-wheel-drive cars). If in doubt, check the owner's manual or ask the auto parts clerk to help you identify the oil drain plug.

oil drain plug   oil filter

Here's an alternative location for an oil drain plug, at the front of the engine's oil pan on a rear-wheel-drive car.

6. Carefully remove the drain plug so the hot oil that begins flowing falls into the drain pan and not onto your hands. Allow all the oil to drain out of the pan before proceeding. While you're waiting, inspect the drain plug and washer for damage, replacing as needed.

7. Once the oil is completely drained out of the oil pan (this may take 5 to 10 minutes), carefully move the drain pan under the filter to catch oil when the filter is removed, your next step.

8. To remove the oil filter, slip the oil filter wrench over the end of the filter until it is near the engine. Then move the filter handle until it cinches down on the filter and begins turning it counterclockwise, or off. Unscrew the filter cartridge by hand, then carefully tip it so hot oil in the filter flows into the drain pan. Once drained, wipe excess oil from the filter connection.

There are various types of oil filter wrenches, sized for specific filters. Make sure you get the one recommended by your auto parts retailer for the filter you are installing.

Technician's Tip

What if you just can't get the old filter off? Wearing protective goggles and gloves, pierce the oil filter with a long screwdriver as close to its base as possible. Then rotate the screwdriver to turn the filter counterclockwise. If there's sufficient room, you can also use a hammer and chisel to turn the filter's base counterclockwise. Just a few taps will usually break the seal. Remember that the filter's body is thin metal and can tear easily—and cut you.

9. Make sure that all oil has drained from the pan and the filter connection, then replace the drain plug and tighten with a wrench. To make sure your filter gets the best seal, pour a small amount of oil on your index finger and rub it on the rubber gasket on the filter's base.

10. Replace the filter, carefully twisting it clockwise on the center shaft, tightening it by hand only. Some filter manufacturers recommend one turn after the gasket makes contact with the engine surface. Don't use the filter wrench. (The filter container is relatively thin and can be crushed or punctured. Oops!)

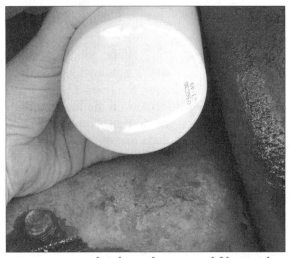

Screw on and tighten the new oil filter with your hand. Don't use a filter removal wrench!

11. Once you're *positive* that the drain plug and filter have been properly replaced, jack up the car slightly and carefully remove the stands. Slowly lower the jack and remove it from under the car.

12. Remove the oil filler cap (if not already off) and insert the oil funnel in the opening, making sure that it will not leak when oil is poured.

Here's where your collection of inexpensive automotive funnels comes in handy again.

Remove the filler cap and insert the funnel.

13. Make sure you know exactly how much oil is required to fill the engine *with the filter installed*. Then remove the cap or use an opener to open the first can of oil and carefully pour it into the oil funnel. Allow all of the oil to drain from the container before removing. How much is enough? Your owner's manual or parts store clerk will tell you.

Make sure you know and have set aside the correct number of quarts of oil needed for an oil change with filter. Pour the first quart slowly.

14. Continue pouring oil into the funnel until the recommended oil capacity is reached. If a partial quart of oil is required, estimate conservatively as you pour in the last amount. It's easier to add oil than to remove it.

15. Reinstall the oil filler cap and wait a few minutes until all oil has drained to the bottom of the engine. You can spend the time cleaning up.

Carefully reinstall the oil filler cap and clean up any excess oil that has spilled (hopefully, none).

 Auto Alert _____

Don't overfill the oil! Excess oil can gum up spark plugs or damage oil seals and cause you to visit your mechanic—and your banker.

16. Use the oil dipstick to check the oil level as described in Chapter 5. If it's within the "full" range, replace the dipstick and start the engine to warm up the oil.

dipstick tube

Make sure the warm oil is up to the "full" or "max" mark on the dipstick. If not, add as needed.

17. Let the engine cool for a few minutes while the engine oil drains to the oil pan. Then recheck the oil level and, if needed, add oil to the "full" line.

18. Pat yourself on the back for a job well done—after you've washed your hands!

To see how gooky oil can become, dip your finger (au natural or gloved) into the old oil collection pan and take a look. Comparing its color, texture, and smell to new oil can tell you about your engine's condition.

Checking the old oil can show you what your engine's been doing. Water or coolant indicates a leak in the engine. Metallic particles suggest excessive wear. If in doubt, take a sample to your auto parts house for a second opinion.

You're done! In three months you'll change oil and filter again—plus tackle semiannual maintenance, coming up in the next chapter.

The Finish Line

◆ Oil is your car's lifeblood; fortunately, changing oil is an easy job that can keep your car running longer.

◆ Plan to change your car's oil and filter every 3,000 to 5,000 miles or every three months, whichever occurs first.

◆ With the right tools you can change your car's oil and filter in less than a half-hour for less than $15.

◆ Always work safely, using jack stands to support the car whenever you work underneath it.

Start Your Engines ...

- ◆ Why you should rotate your car's tires
- ◆ Step-by-step instructions for rotating tires
- ◆ Take a look at your brake system
- ◆ Checking out your car's steering and suspension

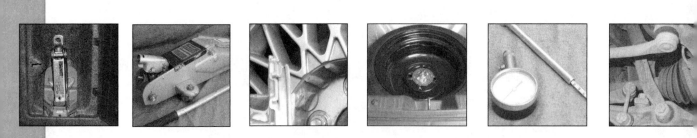

Twice-a-Year Maintenance

Chapter 7 offered step-by-step illustrated instructions for changing your car's oil and filter. It's the most popular car care task that owners can easily do. But wait, there's more!

Twice a year (every other quarter) you can also perform other vital maintenance procedures that will keep your car on the road longer. They're just as easy as an oil and filter change—especially if you do them at the same time. What are they? Maintaining tires, brakes, and suspension.

Rotating Tires

Most tire and car manufacturers recommend that you rotate tires every 7,500 miles. Why? Because tires don't wear evenly. Even properly inflated tires wear differently in different locations on the car. Front tires get wear from turns that back tires don't get. The front suspension system may wear the tire's tread differently from the rear suspension system. To get the most wear out of all tires, consider rotating them regularly.

There are two types of tire rotations depending on what type of tires are mounted on your car. Original-equipment tires typically are nondirectional, meaning they don't really care which wheel they're mounted on. Directional or unidirectional tires must stay on the same side of the car as originally mounted, back to front and front to back. How can you tell which type of tire your car has? The side of the tire will have the word "rotation" and arrows indicating the direction the tires are designed to roll. The arrows point toward the front of the car.

Nondirectional tires are typically rotated in one of three patterns, depending on the type of car:

◆ Front-wheel-drive cars rotate front tires to the back and the back tires to the *opposite* front.

◆ Rear-wheel-drive cars rotate front tires to the *opposite* back and back tires to the front.

◆ Four-wheel-drive cars rotate front tires to the *opposite* back and back tires to the *opposite* front.

Confused yet? Check your car's owner's manual for recommendations on rotating the original and exact replacement tires. Some tire technicians say that it really doesn't matter as much on newer cars.

Wear Indicators

As you rotate your car's tires, check tire pressure to make sure each tire is properly inflated (the recommended tire pressure is stamped on the side of the tire). Look for wear, too. Most modern tires have wear indicators, colored strips on the tread that are only visible when the tread depth is too shallow for safety. Ask your tire supplier whether your tires have wear indicators and how to read them.

Here's the process for rotating nondirectional tires:

1. Make sure the engine is off and that the parking brake is set.

2. Follow the car manufacturer's instructions for using a jack to lift the front of the car until the tires are not touching the ground, then install stands under the frame. (If you're also doing an oil change, you can rotate tires before removing the jack stands.)

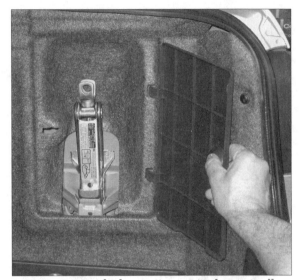

Most cars include a scissors jack, typically found in a side compartment in the trunk.

scissors jack

Use the car's scissors jack or a hydraulic jack to lift the car, then install stands underneath the frame.

Technician's Tip

Some "spare" tires are not intended for use except in an emergency. Your car's owner's manual will tell you which type you have and how to use it.

If you'll be doing other under-the-car work and don't want to mess with using the typically flimsy scissors jack that comes with many cars, consider renting or buying a hydraulic floor jack.

3. Next, lift the rear of the car and securely install stands under the frame. The car is now level and entirely supported by the four stands.

   If you'd rather not put the entire car up on stands, jack up one wheel and replace it with the spare, then move to the next location in the rotation and replace the wheel with the first removed tire. Continue for all four tires and you'll wind up replacing the spare with the fourth tire. Put the spare back in the trunk and you're done. Of course, remember to check air pressure on each tire as it's removed and reinstalled.

4. Use a tire iron or large socket wrench to loosen the nuts (called lug nuts) on each tire, then carefully remove the tire and lay it in front of the wheel. Lay the lug nuts under the edge of the car so they won't get lost before being reinstalled on the same wheel later.

Use a tire wrench, called a tire iron, to loosen lug nuts on the wheels.

Some cars require that you remove a cover to expose the wheel's lug nuts.

If you're driving a pickup truck or motor home with two rear wheels on each side (called a "dually"), don't attempt to remove and rotate these tires unless you have a heavy-duty jack and jack stands plus lots of muscle (or a pneumatic wrench) to remove these heavy wheels and tires.

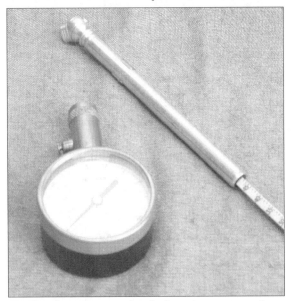

Take this time to check the air pressure in your car's tires, matching them to the car and tire manufacturers' recommendations. If in doubt, ask your favorite tire store for recommended air pressure.

Stop! You can now perform the other two maintenance tasks described in this chapter while the tires are off and *before* they are rotated. Once you've inspected the brakes and the suspension, proceed to the next step in this list.

5. Based on the rotation pattern required for the type of tires your car has, move one tire to its new location. Use the tire lying below the wheel as a ramp to help you move the new tire into place.

6. Turn the tire or wheel so the wheel bolts line up with the holes in the wheel rim, then slip the wheel into place. Put one lug nut on the highest wheel bolt and turn it a few times. Then replace the other lug nuts by hand. (Note: The side of the lug nut that is flat goes toward the outside of the wheel and the side that is wedge-shaped goes toward the wheel.)

7. Tighten all lug nuts on the wheel so that the rim is snug. (You must use a torque wrench to tighten wheel lug nuts.) Once done, grab the front and back edges and wiggle the tire to make sure that it's tightly fastened to the wheel hub.

A torque wrench allows you to control the amount of torque power you apply to tighten a lug nut.

8. Repeat the process for the other wheels and tires, following the rotation pattern suggested by the manufacturer.

9. Jack up the back of the car, carefully remove the stands, then lower the jack so the tires are on the ground. Repeat with the front end of the car.

That's the process. It's the same for changing a flat tire: Jack up the car, install a stand if available (for safety), remove the wheel, replace it with the spare, then remove the stand and the jack.

Spare tires for passenger cars are typically located under the floor in the trunk. They may be located under the bed frame on a pickup truck.

Inspecting Brakes

As you can see, the best time to inspect your car's *brake* system is once you've done all the work of supporting the car and removing the wheels. At that point, a brake inspection takes just a few minutes at each wheel.

 Car Lingo _____

An automotive **brake** converts the car's forward motion (kinetic energy) into heat energy through frictional force applied to the wheels. Excessive use of brakes can make them "hot" and subject to excessive wear or even a fire.

So what's a brake inspection? It's a procedure for checking the brake system's components at each wheel. (You learned how to check the brake's master cylinder and refill fluid in Chapter 6.) You'll be looking for fluid leaks, wear, and foreign objects.

There are two types of brakes used on modern cars: disc and drum. Older cars had only drum brakes. Some newer ones use disc brakes front and back. But most modern cars use disc brakes on the front and drum brakes on the back of the car. Let's take a quick look at each.

Disc (sometimes called caliper) brakes work similar to the rim brake on a bicycle. The driver presses on the brake pedal and the force is magnified by the hydraulic brake system to squeeze a stationary caliper against the rotating disc. The caliper has a brake pad on it that can be replaced once it's worn.

Drum brakes use the same hydraulic pressure to push convex metal components called brake shoes against the inside surface of a drum that's attached to the rotating wheel.

rotor

caliper (pads inside)

Check your disc brakes for damage to the large round component, called the rotor, and any rocks or debris stuck under the smaller component, called the caliper.

With the wheel off, you can inspect the exterior of the drum and look for dust (indicating shoe wear) or damage.

shock absorber

brake fluid lines

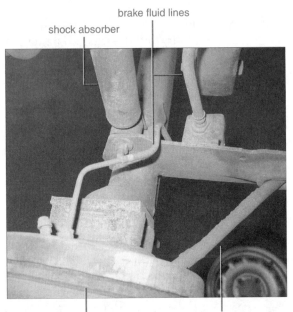

brake drum   parking brake

You can also look behind the drum to see if there are any obvious leaks of hydraulic brake fluid or frayed hydraulic brake lines.

Brakes are relatively simple in function, but a little more complex in design. However, once you've identified the type of brake and how the major parts function, you can easily see how the secondary parts work. Further, you can inspect the parts to see if there are any problems. Chapter 11 will guide you through brake repairs if you want to tackle the job yourself. If not, you'll know how to converse with your brake mechanic.

Once the wheel rim is removed, you can see the major components of disc brakes. However, to inspect drum brakes you must remove the drum, too. To do so, pull the drum toward you. Because of the force required to remove a drum, some consumers choose not to inspect the inside of drum brakes.

What should you be looking for?

◆ Look behind the wheel hub to find where the hydraulic brake line comes in and inspect the line for obvious wear or damage. (A mirror can be used to see behind the wheel without crawling around.)

◆ Look behind the wheel for wet or slick spots that could indicate leaking hydraulic fluid. If necessary, use a wrench to carefully tighten any fittings.

◆ Clean brake surfaces with a clean rag, clean paint brush, or compressed air. (Due to dust particles stirred up by compressed air, wear a mask and goggles.)

◆ Inspect brake surfaces for obvious wear or damage. (An asphalt pellet from a newly paved road can lodge between brake surfaces and cause noises, for example.)

Inspecting Steering and Suspension

Before reinstalling the wheels and tires, you can also inspect the major *steering* and suspension components on your car in a matter of minutes. The steering system turns your car. Suspension is the system that helps smooth out bumps in the road. Most of these components are located behind the wheels, so take a few minutes now to familiarize yourself with them and check their condition.

Steering parts include the tie rods and joints that connect the steering column to the wheels. Another important part is the *rack and pinion* or the *pitman arm* that translates the steering gear's rotation to side-to-side movement.

Car Lingo

Steering transfers the turning movements of the steering wheel to the car's front wheels. Modern cars typically use **rack-and-pinion** steering systems that use one gear across another to transfer movement. Older cars use **pitman-arm** steering that relies on a lever to move the steering components.

What should you inspect on the steering system?

◆ Follow the connection from the back of each front wheel to the steering column, looking at each component for obvious damage or wear.

◆ Look at each joint to see if the rubber components are damaged. (Chapter 11 outlines repairs or how you can describe the problem to your mechanic.)

◆ If your car's owner's manual suggests lubricating steering fittings, you can do so with a lube gun (purchased at an auto parts store; instructions included).

Your car's suspension system absorbs the bumps or shocks of the road. So the major component is called the shock absorber. It's a cylinder with one end connected to the car's frame. The other end is connected to the suspension.

In addition, a large spring absorbs some of the road's shock. The spring may be in the shape of a coil or, on the rear of some cars, a group of slightly bent leaves called a leaf spring. Inspecting springs typically means making sure that they are securely connected to the car at each end of the spring. A broken spring bracket can keep the spring from doing its job.

coil spring

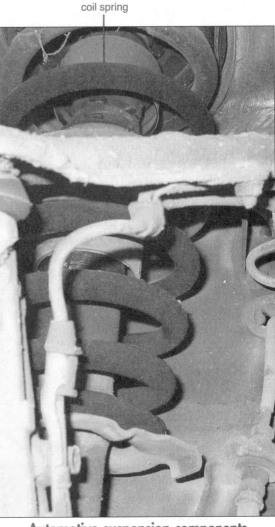

Automotive suspension components
include coil springs.

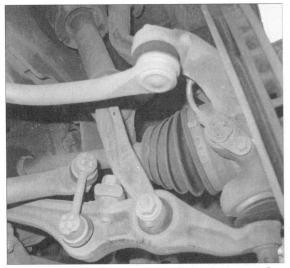

Inspect all major connections to the rear of
the wheel, typically the steering components.

shock absorber

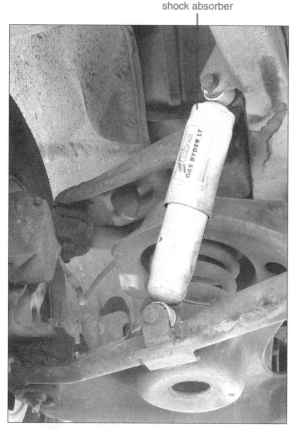

Inspect the shock absorber for damage, especially hydraulic leakage that would suggest internal damage.

Hey, by now you're getting to be quite the mechanic, aren't you? In this chapter you've tackled jobs that most folks avoid. And, hopefully, you've discovered that those jobs really aren't that tough. In fact, you're ready to take on some more maintenance. Once a year you can add to your repertoire with the easy car care tasks coming up in the next chapter.

The Finish Line

◆ Rotating your car's tires every six months can dramatically extend their useful life—and your safety on the road.

◆ Changing a flat tire involves some of the same steps as rotating the tires.

◆ Inspect your car's brakes twice a year to help you make sure they're in good shape for another six months.

◆ Taking a few minutes to check out your car's steering and suspension systems can keep expensive roadside repairs to a minimum.

Start Your Engines ...

- ◆ What's involved in annual car maintenance

- ◆ Why it's important to replace your air filter

- ◆ Inspecting fuel and brake lines, and your car's exhaust system

- ◆ A few other adjustments you can make (or hire someone to do)

Chapter 9

Every-Year Maintenance

Today's cars require so much less maintenance than dad's car. However, when something goes wrong on today's car it takes a cosigner to get it repaired. That's a big reason why you or some other trustworthy soul should make sure that required car maintenance gets done.

Once a year, maintenance gets a little more technical. Some of the jobs, like replacing the air filter, are relatively easy. Others, like adjusting valves, are tougher, especially as the number of valves on modern engines increases. This chapter will show you what is typically done for annual maintenance so you can decide what's a do-it-yourself job and what isn't.

The Annual Checkup

Just as most of us need to get an annual physical checkup, so do our cars. However, the similarities end there. Not all cars are created equally—nor are they built by the same manufacturer. One model may require extensive maintenance once a year or every 12,000 to 15,000 miles, while another doesn't. One car spends life in the fast lane while another travels only to the market on weekends.

The point is that your mileage may vary. Your car's manufacturer may recommend that spark plugs be changed once a year, while another may say two or even three or more years is fine.

Having said all that, here's what I'll be covering in this chapter:

◆ Replacing the air filter
◆ Inspecting the cooling system
◆ Inspecting fuel lines
◆ Inspecting brake lines
◆ Inspecting the exhaust system
◆ Adjusting the parking brake
◆ Adjusting valves

Most of these jobs can be done with basic wrenches and screwdrivers. Adjusting valves, however, requires feeler gauges—thin strips of metal of specific thickness that measure the exact distance between two parts. You can buy feeler gauges for about $2 at your auto parts store.

Replacing the Air Filter

During a year, your car may pull in 7,000 to 10,000 gallons of air to be mixed with gasoline as the engine's fuel. You certainly don't want dust and bugs inside your engine where they can cause problems. So to protect the engine, your car has an air filter. Early cars didn't have air filters and later ones were relatively crude. However, today's major-brand air filters are efficient and require no maintenance other than periodic replacement.

Technician's Tip

I'm covering replacing the air filter under the "annual maintenance" list, but if you live in a dusty location or drive where the air has lots of particulates (including pollen), you should change your car's air filter more frequently—two or even three times a year. Air filters are relatively inexpensive and the job is easy. A clean air filter can quickly pay for itself in fuel savings. By the way, don't think you can just blow out the debris on the old filter and replace it. Blowing out debris requires compressed air, which will damage the paper filter inside.

On old cars the air filter was located above the carburetor. Today's cars are shorter, so the air filter is typically located near the front of the engine compartment where it can pull air in from the outside as the car moves down the road. Look for a rectangular plastic box.

air filter housing

The air filter housing is typically easy to find under the hood. For most newer cars, look to the left or right side of the engine. On older cars with carburetors, the air filter will be above the carburetor near the center of the engine.

Once you locate the air filter housing, here's how to change the filter:

1. Remove the clips or unscrew the screws holding the top of the air filter in place.

Screws or clips (shown) attach the top of the filter housing and must be removed to access the filter.

2. Carefully lift the filter cover (there may be more clips or screws) out of the way to expose the old air filter.

Lift the filter housing cover to expose the filter element.

3. Lift out the air filter, then wipe or vacuum out the housing and cover. Inspect the cover, housing, and air tubes for blockage or cracks and repair as needed. (You don't want dirty air coming in the housing after the point it was supposedly filtered.)

Lift the filter element to remove it. You can see the dirt and debris this filter has stopped from entering the car's engine.

4. Match the old filter to the new unit to verify that it's an exact replacement, then install the new filter. (Air filters vary; check the owner's manual or ask at the auto parts store for the correct air filter for your car.) Note that some air filters have an up side; if in doubt, install it exactly as the old filter was installed.

Replace the filter element and reinstall the air filter housing.

5. Replace the filter cover and the clips or screws.

6. To continue your education, inspect the old filter for quality and whether it seemingly did its job. You may discover (and note in your Car Journal) that one brand of filter seems more efficient than another, or that pollen from nine months ago blocked the filter, probably reducing gas mileage. In that case, change the air filter twice a year or once right after local pollen season ends.

> **Technician's Tip**
>
> Want to save even *more* time and money? Buy a year's worth of oil filters at the same time (two or three) when you see them on sale. Not only will you save a few bucks, you'll also save the time it takes to hunt them down.

Inspecting the Cooling System

About once a month, you've been checking the coolant level in your car (see Chapter 6). Once a year, while you're doing that job, you can perform a closer inspection of the cooling system and make some adjustments.

Your car's cooling system uses a water pump (or, more correctly, a coolant pump) to circulate a mixture of antifreeze and water through the engine to reduce heat buildup. Aluminum engines don't need as much coolant to keep them in a safe temperature range as older iron engines. However, they *must* have coolant or they will be damaged quickly.

A fan pulls air through the *radiator* to lower the temperature of the coolant inside. But how does the coolant get from the radiator to inside the engine? A rubber hose at the bottom of the radiator carries coolant to the engine. Another rubber hose at the top of the radiator draws the coolant from the engine.

> **Car Lingo**
>
> A **radiator** is an important automotive component that transfers excess engine heat to the surrounding air via a liquid (coolant) and a fan.

Inspecting the cooling system becomes obvious. Here are the steps:

1. Inspect the radiator on both sides to see if there's any damage or to remove any leaves that may be blocking the cooling surface. (Actually, you can perform this quick check anytime.)

Your car's radiator is typically located in the engine compartment behind the front grill. If your car has an air-cooled engine, you can skip this step.

upper hose

lower hose

Check the radiator's top and bottom hoses for firmness and obvious damage or leaks.

2. Inspect the top hose for obvious damage (bulges) or leaks (coolant has a light-green tint) and tighten the two clamps with a screwdriver. If the hose requires replacement, you'll first need to drain the radiator of all coolant (see Chapter 11).

3. Inspect the bottom hose for damage or leaks and tighten the two clamps with a screwdriver. (You can more easily do this while your car is already up on stands for your car's quarterly tire rotation and underside inspection, covered in the previous chapter.)

4. Make sure the engine is cool, then remove the radiator cap (push down and turn counterclockwise) to inspect the coolant for level and color. The cap is designed to maintain the coolant under a specific pressure, so some cautious folks replace the cap once a year to forego any problems—the caps cost much less than a damaged engine!

Remove the radiator cap to inspect the coolant. If necessary, test the coolant as covered in Chapter 6.

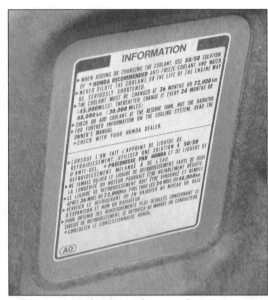

Information about coolant replacement may be found on a plate under the car's hood. If it's not, check the car's owner's manual or service manual, or ask your favorite parts clerk.

Inspecting Fuel Lines

Fuel lines are hoses with metal fittings that bring gasoline (or diesel) from the tank to the engine. Some fuel systems are pressurized. All use a fuel pump to deliver the fuel. So it's especially important that the fuel lines are in top condition. Once a year, your job is to inspect the lines at each connection to make sure there is no damage or leaks. Here's how to do it:

1. Starting at the fuel tank, inspect the fuel line for obvious damage, leaks, or the smell of gasoline. Because gasoline evaporates quickly, you may not see drips. However, you may see discoloration on the garage floor or pavement below where fuel has leaked out. (Note that the fuel pump on some cars is near the tank while on others it is near or on the engine. A few have filters built into the fuel tank requiring tank removal to change the filter—a task best left to experts!)

fuel rail   fuel line

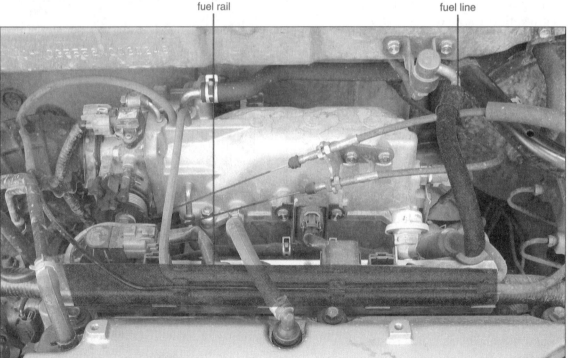

Sometimes the fuel line is difficult to find. Look for the fuel injection system or carburetor on the engine and see what metal tubes feed it.

2. Follow the fuel line toward the engine. Note that fuel lines are typically attached to and follow the car's under-frame. Inspect for damage or leaks. If in doubt, press a dry cloth to a suspected leak to see if the cloth becomes wet.

3. Inspect the fuel line as it comes into the engine compartment and enters the fuel filter. Some car manufacturers recommend replacing the fuel filter once a year, while others suggest every two years. Because fuel filters typically cost just a few dollars, be on the safe side and consider replacing it once a year. To do so, check your car's owner's manual for the specific location (probably near the rear of the engine compartment) and instructions for removal (you'll find either a clamp connection or two nuts securing the filter). Be careful, because pressurized fuel systems require special instructions for replacing a fuel filter.

4. Follow the fuel line to where it connects to the fuel injection system (or carburetor on older cars) atop the engine. Check all fittings for a secure connection and inspect for obvious leaks. To replace lines, follow the service manual for your car or take it to a mechanic for further work.

If you suspect problems with your fuel system, take it to a qualified mechanic for a fuel pressure test, as shown here.

Inspecting Brake Lines

Your car's brake system uses hydraulic fluid to magnify your foot's pressure to stop the car. In Chapter 6, you learned how to check brake fluids. You're now going to inspect the lines and parts that do the actual work.

As with fuel lines, brake lines should have tight fittings and no leaks. Once your car is up on stands for regular maintenance, inspecting the brake lines is an easy task.

Numbered steps aren't necessary here. You simply follow the line from behind each brake to the master cylinder in the engine compartment. You'll probably do this as you inspect brakes (see Chapter 8) and inspect fuel lines (covered earlier in this chapter). You're looking not only for loose fittings and obvious leaks, but also for damaged lines. Road debris such as large rocks can smack the underside of your car, possibly denting hydraulic lines and diminishing fluid flow to one or more brakes. Not good! Inspect, tighten, and replace (or have replaced) as needed.

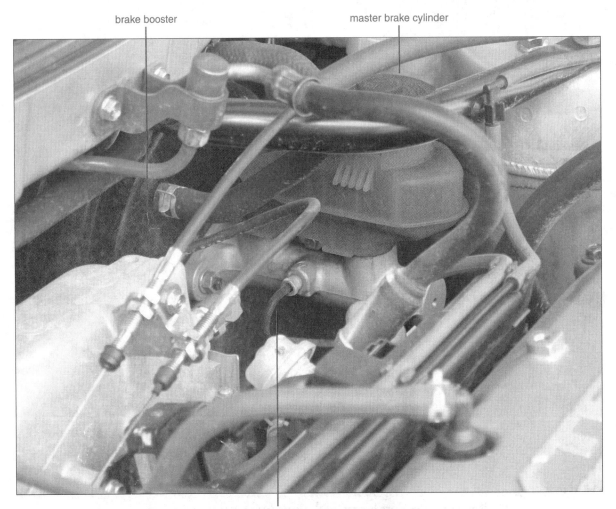

brake booster · master brake cylinder · brake line

The master brake cylinder is typically at the rear of the engine compartment when you're looking at the compartment from the front. It magnifies foot pressure from the brake pedal to move the brake cylinders and components at each wheel.

master cylinder   brake booster

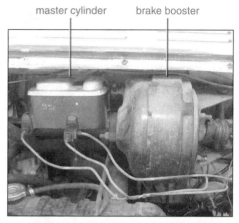

Here's a brake master cylinder, booster, and brake lines on an older van.

While you're inspecting things, look at your car's antilock brake system (ABS) controller, if equipped. It's usually near the master brake cylinder in the engine compartment. Check for fluid leaks and loose connections.

brake line

parking/emergency brake cable

Here, behind a rear wheel, you can see the brake line (left) enter the rear of the drum brake system. The other line (right) is the emergency or parking brake cable.

 Auto Alert

Brakes work until they don't. Taking a few moments to inspect brake lines, parts, and brake fluid level can tell you if something is amiss. Brake line connections typically leak at a connection behind a wheel or at the master cylinder. Because brake fluid is a hydraulic fluid, a leak is easier to spot than a gas or water leak that quickly evaporates. Even if you don't otherwise mess with your brake system, make sure you visually inspect it at least or twice a year.

Inspecting the Exhaust System

Another crawl-around job is inspecting your car's exhaust system. You'll be looking for obvious damage to the exhaust pipe, the catalytic converter, and the muffler. Some cars have a single exhaust system coming off the engine to the rear of the car, while others have a dual exhaust system.

Note that the catalytic converter's job is to cook some of the exhaust emissions so they are less harmful to the environment. The operative word here is "cook," meaning that lots of heat is involved. So make sure the entire exhaust system—but especially the catalytic converter—is cool before attempting an inspection.

muffler   exhaust pipe

catalytic converter

Your car's exhaust system includes the exhaust manifold on the engine, exhaust pipes, catalytic converter(s), muffler(s), clamps, and hangers.

What are you looking for? There may be some road damage to the pipes, converter, or muffler that, unless significant, probably won't stop them from doing their job. However, water is a byproduct of the exhaust process, and water plus metal means rust. So you'll also be looking for holes caused by rust. Noisy mufflers are caused by rust holes. Fortunately, most rust damage is on the lower side of these components where it can more easily be seen from underneath the car.

Here's a typical catalytic converter removed from a car.

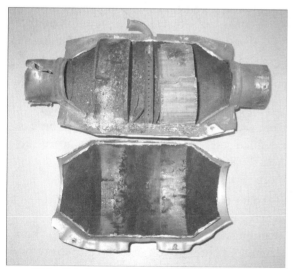

This is what the inside of a damaged catalytic converter looks like. If not replaced, a defective catalytic converter can overheat and cause a fire.

Adjusting the Parking Brake

Your car's parking brake is a handy gadget that lets you park on hills and other sloping surfaces. But wait, it's also an emergency brake that can actually stop your car in a pinch. (Don't try this unless absolutely necessary.) The second function can be a lifesaver if your main hydraulic brakes fail for some reason. That's because, on most cars, the parking/emergency brake system is mechanical. You pull the lever or push on the little pedal and a cable connected to the rear brakes moves the brake shoes or calipers to stop the car.

 Auto Alert _____

Are parking brakes necessary? Only if you park your car! Transmissions, especially older ones, can slip out of gear and move without anyone being present—except maybe a child playing nearby. Get in the habit of setting your parking brake whenever you park, even if it's on a level surface.

Hydraulic brake systems are smarter because they actually adjust themselves as brake surfaces wear out from use. However, mechanical brakes aren't self-adjusting—so you must periodically adjust them. Once a year is about right unless you must frequently park on hills.

Here's how to test a parking brake: While the car is parked on a moderate slope, slowly pull (or push) on the parking brake to determine where in its travel the brake begins to engage and where it is totally engaged. It should begin to engage at about one third of the travel and be fully engaged at two thirds of travel. (Manufacturer's suggestions vary, however.) The brake needs adjustment if it is not fully engaged *before* the end of its travel.

Here's how to adjust the *typical* parking brake:

1. With the car securely up on stands, locate the parking brake adjustment. It's probably located directly under the parking brake and underneath the car.

2. With a wrench or screwdriver (depending on requirements), move the parking brake adjustment. To tighten the brake, turn the adjustment to remove slack from the line. Measure the adjustment made so that you can make subsequent adjustments.

3. Test the first adjustment. If it's not sufficient, make additional adjustments. Don't overadjust or the parking brake will always be on, damaging your brake system.

Adjusting Valves

Here's where many do-it-yourselfers hire a mechanic. Why? Because *valves* are very sensitive to adjustment. Improper adjustment can dramatically change your gas mileage—or damage the engine. However, the job itself isn't that difficult. So if you're mechanically inclined and want to save quite a few bucks, invest in a shop manual for your model car and have at it.

> **Car Lingo**
>
> A **valve** is an engine component that opens and closes to control the flow of liquid, gas, or vacuum. Most commonly, the intake valve(s) lets the fuel-air mixture into the engine and the exhaust valve(s) lets combusted gases out of the engine. Smaller engines have more than one of each valve in a cylinder to save room in the cylinder head.

As an overview, here's how valves are adjusted on modern cars. Remember that the valve's job is to open and close at exactly the perfect moment so that fuel comes in or exhaust exits the cylinder as designed. A critical component called the camshaft actually does the timing. What you'll be adjusting is the lash or opening between parts.

1. Remove the engine's valve cover (this may require moving some other components depending on the car's design).

   Rotate the engine until the TDC (top-dead-center) mark is under the pointer at the crankshaft pulley.

2. Use a valve feeler gauge to measure the distance between the valve's rocker arm and valve tip. If the distance is not as recommended by the car's manufacturer, loosen or tighten the adjustment nut as needed.

3. Perform the measurement and adjustment for each valve on the engine. Note that intake and exhaust valves have different distances or clearances. In addition, some engines have more than one intake or exhaust valve.

Please don't try to adjust your car's valves from these four steps. The information here is intended solely as an *overview* to the process. Actual instructions (in a service manual) are more specific to your car's requirements.

That's about it for typical yearly maintenance. Some cars have other annual tasks including those that will be covered in the next chapter, Chapter 10, on maintenance every two years. See you there!

valve spring

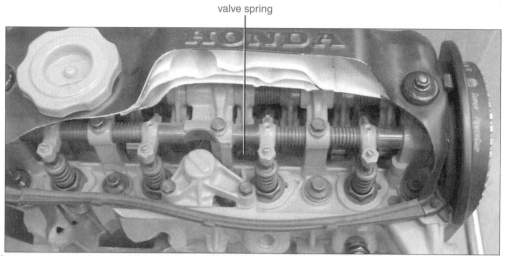

This cutaway of an engine shows a typical valve assembly. The individual valves are adjusted using the nuts on top of each valve.

This cutaway shows a more complex valve assembly. Most car owners don't tackle their car's valve adjustment; however, they can do it with specific instructions in the car's service manual.

The Finish Line

◆ The annual maintenance for your car depends on its make and model, so first check the owner's manual or your parts supplier.

◆ The easiest annual task is to replace the air filter—it's also one of the most important ones.

◆ Once a year, inspect the important fuel and brake lines and the car's exhaust system for potential problems.

◆ Some do-it-yourselfers make annual adjustments to the engine valves and the parking brake—and others hire someone else to do it. It's your choice.

Start Your Engines ...

◆ What kind of maintenance you should do every two years

◆ Replacing your car's spark plugs

◆ Adjusting and replacing engine belts

◆ Replacing coolant—and disposing of it safely

◆ Draining, replacing, and recycling automatic transmission fluid

Chapter 10

Every-Two-Years Maintenance

About every two years (or 30,000 miles), there will be additional car care jobs for your to-do list. Some are relatively easy; others require tools and experience you may not have. In any case, this chapter offers a look at those—and future—maintenance chores that can keep your car on the road longer.

Typical Two-Year Maintenance

As I've emphasized throughout this book, exactly what jobs need to be done when depends on both the manufacturer's service recommendations and how (and where) you drive. For example, a Ford Taurus is scheduled for new spark plugs at 30,000 miles on one model and 100,000 miles on another. However, if you put only 6,000 miles on the car a year, consider changing plugs every 2 years instead of waiting 5 years when you have 30,000 miles on the odometer.

Typical 2-year/30,000 mile service means:

◆ Replacing spark plugs
◆ Inspecting, adjusting, and possibly replacing belts
◆ Replacing coolant
◆ Replacing transmission fluid and filter, if any

Let's take a look at these tasks, step by step.

Replacing Spark Plugs

Replacing *spark plugs* can be an easy chore—or not—depending on how kind the automotive engineers are. Actually, the location and ease of access to spark plugs depends on many engineering factors, including how sleek you want your car to look. Sleek means low, and the space has to come from somewhere. The size of the engine compartment is reduced.

Car Lingo

A **spark plug** is a metal-and-ceramic component that uses electricity to ignite the fuel/air mixture in each cylinder of the engine. A six-cylinder engine has six spark plugs.

Here's a look at the typical automotive spark plug.

Auto Alert

Let your car's engine cool before attempting to remove plugs. It's safer (less chance of getting burned), and it will make removing spark plugs easier. If you're having trouble removing the plugs, carefully spray penetrating oil around the base of the plug and let it soak in. Use caution because penetrating oil is flammable and may ignite with heat; it can also damage nearby electronic parts.

electrode   tip
gap

An electric spark from the car's distributor jumps the gap between the spark plug's electrode and tip. As it does so, it ignites the fuel/air mixture within the cylinder.

So the first trick to replacing spark plugs may be finding the darn things. Fortunately, there are telltale signs. Each cylinder in your car's engine will have a spark plug, and each spark plug requires a wire leading to it. So start by identifying a group of four, six, or eight wires (depending on the number of cylinders) in the engine compartment. Then follow each wire to a spark plug mounted into the engine. Here's the procedure for replacing spark plugs:

1. Use masking tape to mark the wires before removing them from the plugs (so you can put them back on in the correct order). Or use any marking system that you know you'll be able to figure out later.

2. Carefully twist and pull the spark plug wire where it connects to the plug (called the boot) until the boot comes off the plug tip. Make sure you pull on the boot and not the wire or the two may separate.

3. Use a shop rag and small, dry paint brush to clean around the spark plug so debris doesn't fall into the engine when the plug is removed.

4. Use a spark plug wrench to remove the first plug from the engine.

spark plug caps

Follow the wires from the distributor to the spark plug caps (one for each engine cylinder).

socket wrench

extension socket   angle adapter   extension bar

You'll need a spark plug wrench and possibly an extension to remove and install spark plugs.

Remove the spark plug cap. Some caps have an extension such as this one to make access easier.

Insert the spark plug wrench in the hole to grasp the plug, then turn the plug counter-clockwise to remove it.

Remove the spark plug from the engine.

5. Using a wire feeler gauge, check and adjust the *new* spark plug gap according to the manufacturer's recommendation for that engine. The owner's manual or your parts supplier should have that info. (*Always* replace a spark plug with the same make and model unless advised otherwise by a competent auto parts clerk or mechanic.)

graduated feeler gauge

This is a circular feeler gauge for measuring the gap between the spark plug's electrode and tip. There are also flat and wire feeler gauges available at auto parts stores.

Use the feeler gauge to set the specified gap on the new spark plug before reinstalling it.

Technician's Tip

Lubricate the threads of the spark plug with Never-Seize or a similar lubricant (available from your parts supplier) to make the plugs easier to remove the *next* time.

6. By hand, screw the new plug into the spark plug hole until the plug comes in contact with the engine. Then use the socket wrench to tighten the plug two thirds of a turn. (If you have a torque wrench, it's preferred to tighten the plug to the torque value recommended by the car's manufacturer. However, the procedure described here is adequate.)

7. Inspect the spark plug wire and boot for damage, replacing as a unit if needed. Otherwise, place the boot on top of the plug and press firmly.

8. Repeat this process to replace the other spark plugs.

Go Platinum!

Platinum plugs are high-quality spark plugs with platinum tips that last longer than conventional plug tips. Why doesn't every car require platinum plugs? They are about twice as expensive as regular spark plugs. Why do some cars require them? Because the spark plugs are located where they are difficult to replace, it makes good sense to replace them less frequently. The difference in cost is typically less than $2 per spark plug. If you really don't like changing spark plugs, go platinum and do it less frequently.

Adjusting Belts

Accessory belts apply the engine's rotation to turn other components. Depending on the design of your car, these belts may be used to power a coolant pump and fan, alternator, or air conditioner compressor. On some cars, a single belt wraps around all of these accessories like a serpent, so it's called a serpentine belt.

Car Lingo

An **accessory belt** is a continuous reinforced rubber component that connects and transfers power between the engine and various accessories such as the coolant pump, alternator, air conditioner compressor, and power steering pump. A car may have more than one accessory belt by design. A timing belt connects the crankshaft and camshaft, synchronizing or timing their rotation.

Modern engines include a variety of belts that use the engine's power to drive the alternator, air conditioning compressor, smog devices, and other components.

Here's an under-the-car look at the various belts that a rear-wheel-drive car uses.

Check the condition of the serpentine and adjust or replace as needed, following the car's service manual.

As you can imagine, these reinforced belts get lots of action—and lots of wear. And when they fail, your car can quickly become damaged. Because of all the different accessory belt configurations, I'll describe replacement in general terms. Refer to your car's owner's manual or service manual for specifics.

1. Look at the front of the engine to determine what accessory belts the engine has. Make a drawing of them identifying what accessories they drive. (Some accessory belts will require that covers or brackets be moved first.)

2. To remove most accessory belts, look for and loosen the accessory's adjustment. It's typically located on a bracket that attaches the accessory to the engine. Loosen and move the accessory only enough to remove the belt, carefully watching and recording how the belt comes off.

Some components have a sliding adjustment nut as part of the mounting.

adjustment bolt

Other components have a small adjustment nut on the unit.

3. Hold the old belt up to the new one to make sure that both are of the same size, width, thickness, and inner edge design. (Allow for minor stretching and wear of the old belt, however.)

4. Carefully thread the new belt over the pulleys following the pattern of the old belt. Once in place, tighten the accessory adjustment according to the car manufacturer's specifications. In most cases, the manufacturer will suggest a specific amount of slack in the belt.

5. Start the car and carefully view (*don't touch!*) the moving belt to make sure it's operating correctly.

Replacing Coolant

Coolant, like everything else on a car, wears out with use and time. So it makes sense to replace coolant periodically. Many car manufacturers recommend coolant be replaced with new stuff about every two years or 30,000 miles.

Replacing coolant is relatively easy. Getting rid of the old stuff isn't. For most cars, removing coolant means putting an appropriate container underneath the radiator and opening a small valve that allows the coolant to flow out. Once that's done, you close the valve and refill the radiator and reservoir with coolant. (Refer to the car's owner's manual for capacity and mixture information.)

Also, it's a good idea to replace the radiator cap when you change coolant. A cap costs just a few dollars. Its job is to keep coolant adequately pressurized, a relatively important task.

Technician's Tip _____

Check your car's shop or owner's manual for specific instructions on replacing coolant. Some models require that air be purged from the cooling system because the engine is higher than the radiator.

Because most types of antifreeze are poisonous to animals (just a small amount can kill a cat or dog) and may also harm small children, dispose of it properly. The best method is to pour it back into empty antifreeze containers and take it to a hazardous waste recycling center. *Never* pour it down a household drain!

Chapters 6 and 9 include photos of working on the cooling system.

Replacing Transmission Fluid

If you're a die-hard do-it-yourselfer, get out your car's service manual and follow instructions for replacing automatic transmission fluid *and* filter. (Manual transmissions don't need fluid replacement, just periodic refilling through a plug on the side of the tranny.) Draining and replacing automatic transmission fluid isn't that tough a job, but replacing the filter on some cars can be tricky. Basically, here's how the job goes:

1. Place a sufficiently large drain pan under the transmission or *transaxle*, then remove the drain plug to allow all automatic transmission fluid to flow into the pan.

> **Car Lingo**
>
> A **transaxle** is a transmission *and* torque converter, or clutch *and* differential, encased as a single unit on front-wheel-drive cars.

2. Remove the cover on the bottom side of the transmission to expose the transmission filter. As suggested by the car's service manual, remove the filter and replace it with a new unit.

3. Replace the cover gasket with a new one, then replace the transmission pan cover, tightening screws to the manufacturer's recommendations.

4. Dispose of the old transmission fluid, filter, and gasket in an ecologically responsible manner (call your local recycle center for specifics).

transmission pan (from below)

A typical automatic transmission, and pan, as seen from below.

Technician's Tip

Transmission shops use a "dialysis" machine to pump old transmission fluid out while pumping new fluid in. The process takes just a few minutes. However, the tool is too expensive for do-it-yourselfers.

Other Maintenance Jobs

Driving down the highway, you might think that there were only about three models of cars made. Of course, it's not true. In fact, there are about 200 different models now being manufactured. And each year, each model changes slightly from last year's model.

That means each car may have additional maintenance requirements. Air conditioners and ventilation systems like to have their filters changed every couple of years (or more often). Steering components need periodic alignment. Suspension parts such as shocks need replacement. Even no-maintenance batteries can use a cleaning once in a while.

The point here is that doing all the maintenance covered in the last five chapters *won't* guarantee you a trouble-free car. There may be other maintenance recommendations included in your car's owner's manual. However, the biggest and most popular ones are here. Spending an hour or two each month maintaining your car will ensure it a longer life—and your peace of mind.

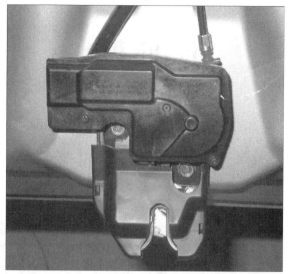

Some cars require a lubrication of various parts every other year. Here's one of the ones that often gets missed: the trunk latch.

The Finish Line

◆ On some cars replacing spark plugs is an easy one-hour job, while on others consider hiring a mechanic—and using highest-quality plugs so you don't have to repeat this job every other year.

◆ Modern cars use lots of belts to power accessories, so every couple of years you'll be adjusting or possibly replacing them.

◆ Coolant gets old, so plan to replace it every two years or as suggested by the car's manufacturer.

◆ Always properly dispose of old coolant and other hazardous materials.

◆ You can drain and replace automatic transmission fluid yourself—or you can hire a professional to do it.

In This Part

Part 3

Illustrated Repairs

Hey, you're getting good at this mechanic stuff. Want to try some more? Good!

This final part offers illustrated instructions for tackling many auto repair jobs you might have thought you'd never be able to do yourself. Since then you've learned that maintenance and repair is easy—if you have someone to show you how. This part covers common mechanical, electrical, body, and interior repairs that you probably can do yourself. And even if you decide to leave the heavy work for a trusted mechanic, you'll know how to get value for your repair-bill dollars.

Congratulations on your progress! Keep up the good work.

Start Your Engines ...

- ◆ Some basic repairs most car owners can handle
- ◆ How to replace major parts on your car
- ◆ Finding the cause and cure for car ills
- ◆ Deciding what you *don't* want to repair yourself

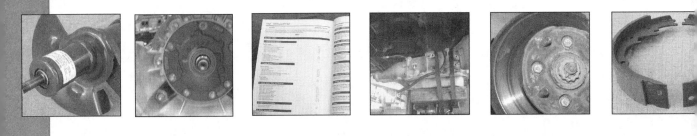

Chapter 11

Easy Mechanical Repairs

A repair typically means fixing something that breaks. By this point, you've gotten so good at maintaining your car that repairs are rarely needed. However, you still must contend with used cars previously owned by folks who minimized or even avoided maintenance. That's when you have to make repairs.

Fortunately, you've learned your way around a car and know what's what. You now also have some experience inspecting, adjusting, and replacing parts *before* they require repair. So the move to required repairs won't be that difficult for you.

This first chapter on repairs covers mechanical problems such as those with the engine, transmission, cooling, suspension, brake, and secondary systems on your car. Obviously, I can't cover *all* mechanical repairs for *all* cars and models in this chapter. For specific instructions, invest in a consumer-level service manual for your car. However, I will show you how to troubleshoot problems and what's involved in making basic repairs that car owners frequently do for themselves. (Even if you elect not to do your own repairs, knowing *how* a repair is made can help you get your money's worth from a mechanic, so keep reading!)

Troubleshooting Problems

What can go wrong on a car? Just about anything! Entire engines have been known to drop out of a car while driving! Fortunately, it happens so infrequently (with *lots* of warning signs) that car owners don't need to worry about it. However, there are many other problems that can ruin a vacation—or a trip to the store.

So let's first talk about warning signs. In the case of an engine falling out, an attentive owner doing her or his car's maintenance would have seen broken supports and noticed that engine mounts were damaged (or missing) and that the engine was shaking hard when idling. Some problems are that obvious but others aren't. The most important skill you can pick up is troubleshooting or learning how to hear what your car is telling you.

Performing automotive maintenance, even just the easy jobs, acquaints you more with your car, how it runs, and what's "normal." It also helps you develop "car logic." You begin to think like a car—or at least a car designer. That's good. So when you hear a rattle near the front of the engine, you can quickly trouble-shoot it to see if the coolant pump is failing—or the engine's going to fall out!

Service manuals typically include a trouble-shooting chart or a chapter on diagnostic procedures. For example:

Engine turns over, but will not start.

- Check fuel level in fuel tank, add fuel if empty. [Hey, it happens!]
- Check battery condition and state of charge.
- Check fuel delivery system.
- Check for contamination (water, rust) in the fuel.
- Check for ignition system failure.
- Check engine management system for a failed sensor or control module.

See how it works? The service manual will give you pages and pages of problems and procedures for troubleshooting your specific car. In fact, reading through the troubleshooting section can help you understand how car systems work together. It's also a cure for insomnia.

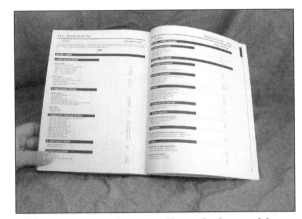

Service manuals typically include trouble-shooting charts for specific make and model cars.

Engine Repairs

Common engine repairs include disassembling, replacing or repairing, and reinstalling primary parts such as pistons, connecting rods, crank-shaft, camshaft, valves, and related parts. Unfortunately, modern engines require precise parts and assembly so most consumers don't repair engine components. Depending on what's needed, it may be less work to buy a new, rebuilt, or used engine and replace the old one. In many cases, that's what professional mechanics do.

What could go wrong with an engine that would require major repair?

- If the engine lacks power, the valves or piston rings could be worn.
- If the engine uses excessive oil, the piston rings or valve guides could be worn. (Note: first check underneath the car to see if there's an easy-to-fix leak.)
- If the engine makes a light clicking noise, the valves may require repair. (First check to make sure that all spark plug wires are working properly; see Chapter 10.)

piston

starter | valve springs

alternator

Cutaway of an older engine to show components.

exhaust valve   intake valve

In case you've wondered, here's what valves look like inside the head or top section of an engine.

◆ If the engine starts but won't run, the timing chain may be loose or broken.

◆ If the engine makes a sharp metallic knock when running, the cause could be the bearings at either end of the connecting rods.

Fortunately, you can test the engine's compression pressure with a *compression tester*. It measures how much pressure a specific cylinder can generate in a single rotation of the crankshaft. You can buy a compression tester for around $20, or rent or borrow one at larger auto supply stores.

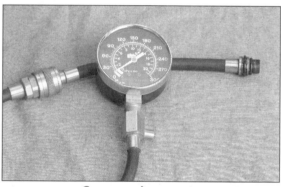

Compression tester.

compression ratio

Typical engine tune-up specifications chart including the compression ratio.

Car Lingo

Compression ratio is the ratio between the space in a cylinder when the piston is at the bottom of travel and at the top of travel. A 7:1 compression ratio means the space in the cylinder is seven times larger when the piston is fully down than when it is fully up, called top dead center or TDC. A **compression tester** measures the *actual* compression within a cylinder. If the engine is designed for 7:1 but the tester shows 6:1 compression ratio, there is a leak of compression within the cylinder, usually around the piston.

Here are the steps for testing the engine:

1. Remove all spark plugs and insert the tester in the spark plug hole per the manufacturer's directions. (Some engine manufacturers require that the gasoline throttle be fully open as well by pressing on the gas pedal or by manually moving the throttle linkage.)

2. Remove the spark plug coil main wire so the engine *won't start* when you perform step 3.

3. Use the ignition to *carefully* rotate the engine at least four revolutions (about one second).

4. Read and write down the compression test results.

5. Replace the spark plug, remove another, and repeat the test.

6. When done, compare the compression test results to the engine manufacturer's data to determine normal operating range and for suggestions of causes and solutions.

valve assembly cover

head

This engine is getting a new head.

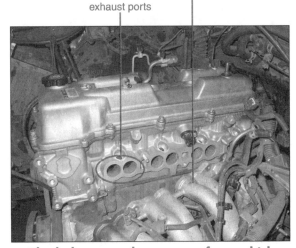

exhaust manifold

exhaust ports

The holes are exhaust ports from which exhaust gases are taken from the engine and into the exhaust system.

Transmission Repairs

Like engines, manual and automatic transmissions are typically replaced rather than repaired if the problem is big. Fortunately, there are tests you can perform on automatic transmissions. In addition, there are linkage adjustments for manual and automatic transmissions to make things better. If necessary, automatic transmissions can be adjusted without removing them from the car. Beyond that, call a number of transmission shops for comparative rates—and make sure your credit card limit is high.

Just a reminder: A transmission for front-wheel-drive cars is combined with the differential, technically referred to as a transaxle. But I'm going to be stubborn and call them transmissions.

Repairing a manual transmission starts with adjusting linkage. Linkage links the shifter with the transmission's gears. Here again, refer to the specific car's owner's manual because just about every car made since the last major war has its own unique linkage system. Having said that, most are fairly similar. Typically, linkage is adjusted by finding and moving the nut on an adjustment rod located near the transmission. Staring at the adjustment for a minute or two—and maybe asking someone to move the shifter through the gears slowly as you watch—will teach you how the linkage works. It may also enlighten you on why it doesn't.

Automatic transmissions, too, have linkage. And most linkage systems have adjustments somewhere near the side of the transmission. However, parts inside an automatic transmission, called bands, may require adjustment as well. This is why automatic transmission specialists go to school. If you're a brave soul, follow instructions in your car's service manual (preferably the professional version) for adjusting an automatic transmission.

The transmission is being replaced in a shop using a special transmission jack.

This is the bell housing or front end of an automatic transmission.

Fortunately, manual and automatic transmissions are a commodity. That means you can replace your old, tired tranny with a new, slightly used, or rebuilt transmission. Removal is relatively easy once the car has sufficient room under it to lower the transmission. It will be attached on one end to the engine with bolts and on the other end to the transaxle differential or to the driveshaft, also with bolts.

Note that front-engine transaxle cars deliver power to the front wheels through CV, or constant velocity, joints. CV joints wear out more frequently than transmissions, so look to these first when you think the car may be having transmission problems. To protect CV joints, most have a sealed rubber cover called a boot that can leak and shorten the joint's life. So inspect the CV joints while you're under the car for maintenance.

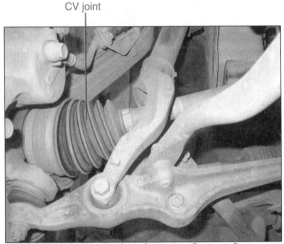

CV joint

Depending on the design of your front-wheel-drive car, accessing and repairing the CV joint can be relatively easy.

Cooling System Repairs

Repairs to the engine's cooling system typically mean replacing the coolant pump, the fan, or the radiator. The coolant pump and fan are usually replaced as a unit by draining coolant from the engine, removing the pump belt, and disconnecting the pump from the engine.

The simplest and most common repair to cooling systems is replacing the *thermostat*.

Car Lingo

A **thermostat** is a valve that opens and closes based on temperature, regulating the flow of coolant in an engine. Thermostats have a specific temperature range, called a **set point**, at which they open or close to keep the coolant's temperature within the designated range.

Replacing the thermostat on your car may be easy or difficult, depending on how the engine was designed. On most cars, the thermostat is located inside a metal housing between the engine and the radiator's top hose. So replacement requires that you drain coolant from the system, remove the hose, remove the housing, and finally remove the thermostat. Install a new one in reverse order. Make sure that you install an exact replacement thermostat because they have different temperature *set points*.

Modern radiators are much smaller than their granddaddies, so removal should be easier. However, because of tight clearances in modern engine compartments, radiator removal and replacement may require moving everything else. The usual steps are …

1. Drain the cooling system.
2. If your car is equipped with an automatic transmission, disconnect its coolant lines from the radiator.
3. Loosen the radiator hose clamps and detach the hoses.
4. If the cooling fan is attached to the radiator, remove it.
5. Loosen and remove bolts holding the radiator to its frame.
6. Remove any other components that are attached to or in the way of removing the radiator.

7. Carefully lift the radiator from the frame.

8. Reinstall the radiator and coolant in reverse order.

See Chapters 6 and 9 for additional photos of the cooling system.

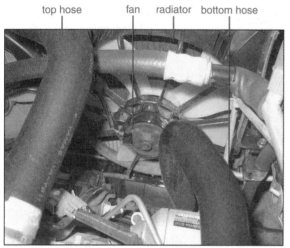

top hose   fan   radiator   bottom hose

Here you can see the cooling system radiator, fan, and hoses.

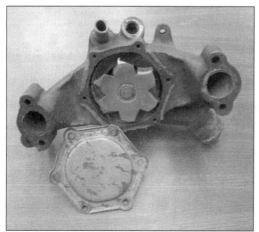

Here's a coolant pump removed from a car. It pumps coolant (antifreeze and water) between the engine and radiator. The plate is removed to show the pump blades.

Steering and Suspension Repairs

Steering systems, too, require specialized knowledge and tools for many repairs such as replacing gearing, rods, and joints. However, there are one or two jobs that the handy car owner can do. One is to replace *shock absorbers* and/or *struts.*

> **Car Lingo**
>
> A **shock absorber** is a sealed cylinder that uses hydraulic fluid to dampen a wheel's up-and-down movement caused by driving over bumps in the road. A **strut** combines the shock absorber and a dampening spring, typically used on front-wheel-drive cars.

The function of shock absorbers is self-explanatory. However, struts don't strut. They are actually a shock absorber wrapped with a coil spring. Both shocks and struts should be changed as a unit; don't try to repair them.

You can purchase a new shock absorber at your auto parts store.

Here's a brand-new strut ready for installation.

Shocks and struts are vertical members behind each wheel. You'll see them as you inspect or repair your car's brake system. Installation is relatively easy. Carefully loosen and remove bolts at the top and bottom of the unit, then replace them with exact replacement parts.

 Auto Alert _____

You'll be installing springy parts under a car that weighs over a ton. Make sure that the car is securely on stands and that you can safely install the shocks or struts. Otherwise, hire a shock shop to do the work.

rear shock absorber
top connection
bottom connection | spring

Here's a shock absorber installed inside a coil spring behind a front wheel.

top shock absorber bracket

The top of the shock absorber is typically attached to the car's body inside the engine compartment and above the wheels.

Brake System Repairs

Brake repair means replacing components that have failed (oops!) or are about to fail.

Hopefully, brake repair for you means replacing brake components before they wear out. Frankly, it's cheaper to replace brake parts 5,000 miles before needed than 5,000 miles after. If before, the *brake pads* or *shoes* won't cost that much. Replacing damaged discs or drums, however, can be very expensive in both parts and labor.

Car Lingo _____

Brake pads are the replaceable components of disc brakes, most often used on the front axle of cars. **Brake shoes** are the replaceable components of drum brakes, most often used on the rear axle of cars. Older cars used brake drums and shoes on all wheels.

In a nutshell, here's how disc brake pads are replaced:

1. Safely jack up the car and place stands under the axles.

2. Remove the wheel covers, if any, then remove the wheel as you would when changing a tire.

3. Inspect the brake caliper, brake pads, wear indicator, disc, and other brake components. If brake pads are worn (most have a wear indicator) or are $\frac{1}{16}$-inch or less thick, replace them with new pads. If the brake disc (rotor) has grooves in it, take it to a brake shop for resurfacing or replace it with a new disc.

Removing a wheel and tire exposes the front disc brake.

Typical disc brake rotor.

Components of a disc brake system.

The old rotor can be turned on a machine to refinish the braking surface.

4. To replace brake pads, use a C-clamp (from an auto parts or hardware store) to push the piston back in the caliper. Remove the bolt(s) holding the caliper and move it aside. *Don't* disconnect the caliper from the brake line.

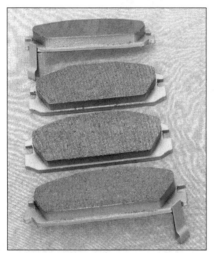

New disc brake pads fit inside the caliper.

disassembled caliper   rotor backing plate

The bare disc brake system awaiting new rotor and pads.

5. Reinstall the disc and hub assembly. If the manufacturer suggests it, also repack the wheel bearings with grease (see the service manual), and reassemble the caliper and other components.

6. Refill the master cylinder with brake fluid and remove (bleed) any air from the brake system if needed. The service manual will show you how.

Drum brakes are repaired in a similar way. Only the parts are different. The two brake shoes press outward on the inside of the drum to stop the car.

shoes   springs

Typical drum brake system.

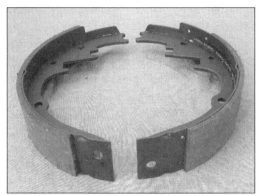

New brake shoes.

You can recharge your air conditioner system (if allowed by state laws) with a refill system available through your auto parts store. The store will know the state regulations, too.

fill valve

Air conditioner systems typically have a fill valve on one of the lines. Be careful because the system is pressurized.

Other Mechanical System Repairs

There are other mechanical systems in your car that will need maintenance or may need repair. They include door and window components (hinges, latches, locks), seats, heater (drawing heat from the engine and cooling system), air conditioner, exhaust, and more.

As you've learned, this book's mantra is: Maintain well and you won't have to repair (as much). The same mantra applies to other mechanical systems. Check your car's owner's manual and service manual for specifics. Newer cars need less lubrication than older ones because they have better plastic joints, but they can still use some silicone grease on seat tracks, door latches, and other frequently used parts.

In addition, keeping your car's coolant system problem-free will do the same for the heating system. As for air conditioning, keep the AC belt on the engine in good condition and well adjusted. Also find (or ask a technician) and check the refrigerant level; most cars have an in-line glass peephole that changes color when refrigerant is low. But don't even *try* to repair the AC system. Too many environmental hazards—and greenhouse laws. Take it to a licensed and certified AC shop.

Finally, the exhaust. It's not quite a mechanical system because it doesn't have moving parts. However, it's certainly not electrical (see Chapter 12) nor part of the car body (see Chapters 13 and 14). So it goes at the end of this chapter. (Actually, it is the exhaust system for the mechanical engine, thus qualifies for current placement.) Whatever.

Again, exhaust system repair really means replacement of worn or nearly worn parts. Exhaust system parts include …

◆ *Exhaust manifold* (back door for the engine's exhaust gases)

Car Lingo

An **exhaust manifold** collects gases from the engine's cylinders and delivers them to the exhaust pipe(s). An intake manifold delivers the fuel/air mixture to the cylinders for burning.

◆ Exhaust pipe(s)
◆ Catalytic converter (converts some of the harmful gases into less harmful elements)
◆ Muffler(s)
◆ Resonator(s)
◆ Lots of little emission-control parts

Because most of these parts are big and have no moving parts, replacement time is easy to calculate. Replace the parts with new ones at the end of their useful life—not after. Using a small hammer or block of wood to tap any of these components (when cold) can tell you if rust is present. Remember, it's easier and cheaper to replace almost-done components at the same time. Fortunately, you can buy bolt-together exhaust system parts. You don't need to be a welder.

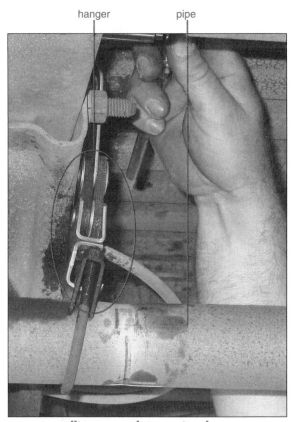

Installing an exhaust pipe hanger.

I've saved the worst for last. Your car probably has an emission-control system (unless it's *really* old) that includes positive crankcase ventilation (PCV) filter and valve, exhaust gas recirculation (EGR) filter and switch, spark delay valve, anti-dieseling device, and a bunch of other parts. They are a family of components that really smart (or sadistic) engineers came up with to help reduce hazardous air emissions from your car. In addition, many new cars have sensors that tell the car's onboard computer (see Chapter 12) whether each component is working properly. If not, the computer responds—and not always in the most owner-friendly way. It may change settings on the car that defy logic.

Here's the point: Check your car's owner's and service manual for the function, location, maintenance, and repair (actually, replacement) of parts in the emissions-control system. Some are relatively simple and cheap, so they can be replaced early. Others are tougher to find and replace. Most car owners (and too many car mechanics) ignore these little parts. My best advice is: don't. Find out how and how often to replace them, and do so. You'll thank me for it!

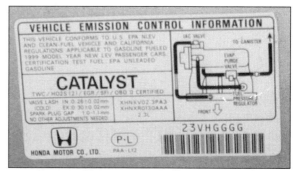

Most modern cars include a plate somewhere under the hood that includes information on the emission control system.

The Finish Line

◆ There are dozens of resources and tools available to you for troubleshooting car problems.

◆ Many major repairs are done by removing and replacing components rather than disassembling them.

◆ Many do-it-yourselfers successfully do their own brake work.

◆ Keep your car well maintained and you won't have to do as many mechanical repairs.

Start Your Engines ...

- ◆ Testing and replacing car fuses
- ◆ Taking good care of your car's battery
- ◆ Replacing other electrical components
- ◆ Using a volt-ohmmeter for testing electronics

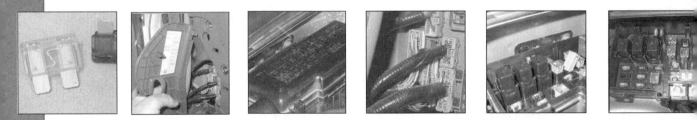

Chapter 12

Easy Electrical Repairs

As you've discovered, part of the engine's power is used to produce electrical power, which then is consumed by the spark plugs, lights, radio, computer, and other paraphernalia. What can you do if the car's electrical system quits working? You can repair it. Yes, you!

This chapter offers step-by-step instructions for curing a number of auto electric ills. You'll learn about fuses, batteries, alternator, computers, lights, the radio, and other electric stuff. It's really quite easy.

Replacing Fuses

The weakest link in an electrical chain is the *fuse*. That's by design. If a circuit gets too much power, you want the fuse to blow rather than the radio, computer, or other gadget. That makes sense. It also makes sense to *first* check the car's fuse system when something electrical quits working.

The interior fuse box is usually located at the side or underneath the dashboard with an easily removed cover.

All wires in the various car systems flow through the fuse box for safety.

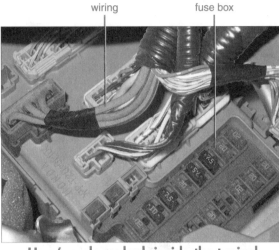

Here's a closer look inside the typical automotive fuse box.

Car Lingo

A **fuse** is an electrical component that's designed to fail first before an electrical overload damages other, more expensive, components. A **fuse box** (or fuse panel) is a group of fuses placed in a relatively convenient location.

The hard part in checking fuses may be finding them. Fortunately, most modern cars put all fuses together in one or two, or (probably) both spots:

◆ Under the hood near the battery (battery, headlight, stoplight, hazard light, horn, heater, air conditioner, and other fuses and relays)

◆ Inside the car under the dashboard (wiper, coil, turn lights, washer, mirrors, fuel pump)

The engine compartment probably has a fuse box to serve components within the compartment.

The engine compartment fuse box can be opened by pressing clips or by removing screws.

Here's a closer look inside a typical engine compartment fuse box.

Technician's Tip

To quickly test fuses, buy a test light (available from auto parts stores), hook the light to a nearby ground connection (see the light's instructions), turn the car's ignition to on, and touch the light's probe to the fuse. If the tester lights up (continuity), the fuse is good. Using this method, you can quickly test many fuses without removing them.

Before you go out and buy extra fuses for emergencies, check the *fuse box*(es) to see what's already there. Many modern cars include a small assortment of spare fuses and maybe even a special tool called a fuse puller. However, you may want to get an extra relay or two because they are cheaper now than when you need them 50 miles from a parts store.

Larger fuses can be carefully pulled by hand; smaller ones require a fuse puller. Fortunately, many car manufacturers include a fuse puller inside the fuse box.

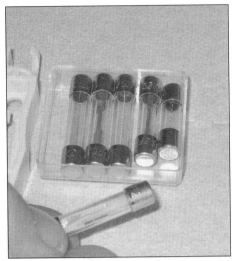

Here's an assortment of tube fuses and a fuse puller.

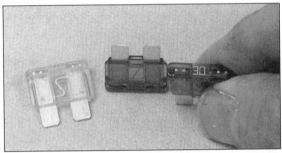

These are blade-type fuses that are easier to remove—and easier to read—than the older style of tube fuses.

How can you check automotive fuses? In most cases, visually. Many fuses are translucent and you can see through the plastic or glass case to determine if there is a break in the fuse. Alternatively, you can use a volt-ohmmeter (VOM or multimeter) to check for continuity. VOMs cost less than $20 at auto parts or electronics stores and are handy for testing lots of electrical things. Instructions typically come with the unit. (A VOM is pictured at the right.)

Testing continuity means testing the resistance between the two ends or prongs of the fuse. The VOM actually sends a small electric charge (from an internal battery) through the fuse and measures whether it comes out the other end. If not, the fuse is blown and must be replaced.

 Auto Alert _____

Remember that you're working with electrical current—be careful working around it so you don't get shocked.

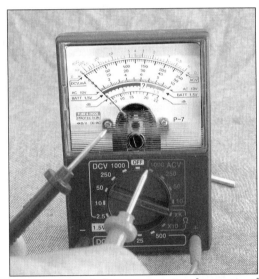

An open circuit (no connection between the probes) is shown on the left side of the VOM display.

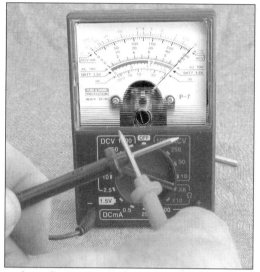

A closed circuit (the probes are touching) takes the needle to the right side of the VOM display.

The VOM display indicates that no electricity is flowing through this fuse; it is blown.

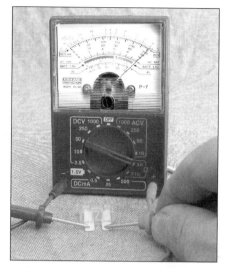

The VOM dial is on the right, signifying continuity. That means electricity can flow through this fuse; it is good.

Solving Battery Problems

Your car's battery is a storage container that gathers electrical power (produced by the engine) and stores it for use by lights, motors, relays, and other gadgets. So it's important that the battery hold the charge.

Fortunately, modern sealed or maintenance-free batteries don't need much service. Other than periodically checking the battery connection (see Chapter 6), there's little to do except wait for the day it should be replaced. Typically, that's every three to five years.

Car Security Code

Many new cars have a security code that must be re-entered into the radio if it's disconnected from the car's battery (as in a theft) or if the battery itself is disconnected. The owner's manual will tell you if this is true for your car and what to do about it. Typically, it means making sure you have the security code *before* you disconnect the battery and re-entering it when you're done.

Here's how to replace a car battery. You can do it yourself:

1. Find the car's battery; it's usually under the hood on passenger's side of the car, but could be just about anywhere.
2. Disconnect the cable from the negative (–) side of the battery first, then the positive (+) side. *Always* disconnect the negative side of the battery first. This disables all electric components and ensures that voltage will not damage the computer(s) or set off the inflatable restraint devices such as air bags.
3. Use a battery brush or rag to clean the terminals.

For most cars, disconnect the negative side of the battery first. That way you won't become the ground when touching something, possibly injuring yourself or some electronics.

Next, remove the positive terminal cable and place it where it will not make contact with metal.

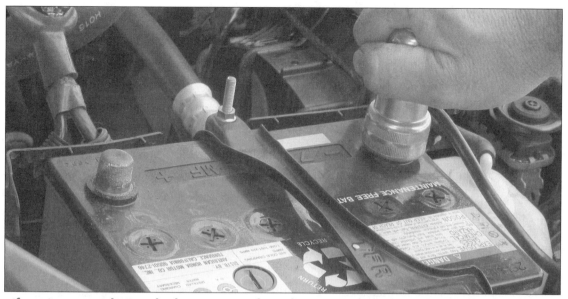

If you're not replacing the battery, just clean the terminals and connections with a brush.

4. Remove the hold-down frame that keeps the battery in place.

5. Attach a battery strap (from an auto parts store) to the two terminals and carefully lift the battery out and away from the car.

6. Inspect the battery holder or tray for corrosion and damage. If needed, clean the area with baking soda and water or a similar cleaner (also from your auto parts store) before installing the new battery. Make sure cleaners or water don't damage nearby electronic equipment. If the battery cables are damaged, replace them as well.

Install the new battery with battery washers that reduce corrosion.

7. Use the battery strap to install the new battery, then reinstall the hold-down frame.

8. Attach the positive cable, then the negative cable to the corresponding battery terminals, placing battery washers on each terminal.

Technician's Tip

Battery terminal rings and lubricants can be used to help neutralize corrosion before it builds up. Your auto parts store has them.

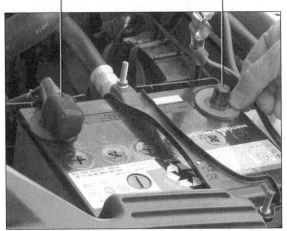

positive (+) terminal   negative (-) terminal

Finally, reinstall the cable to the negative battery terminal.

Replacing the Alternator

The alternator, as you now know, converts some of the engine's power into electric power for storage in the battery. If your car's battery is in good condition and can hold a charge, but doesn't, the alternator may not be doing its job.

Before replacing an alternator, check the car's owner's manual or service manual for specific information about the alternator. For example, many have fuses that can be replaced or breakers that can be reset without replacing the alternator.

As far as the car owner is concerned, an alternator is a commodity. That is, don't even think about repairing it yourself. If it doesn't work, it's best to replace it as a unit. A service manual (or your own hard-earned maintenance experience) can show you how. On most cars, loosen the alternator or accessory belt adjustment and remove bolts that mount it to the side of the engine.

Remember to spend a few dollars more for a quality alternator, because you don't want to have to replace it again next year. Your best bet is one from an OEM (original-equipment manufacturer) or the local new car dealer's parts department.

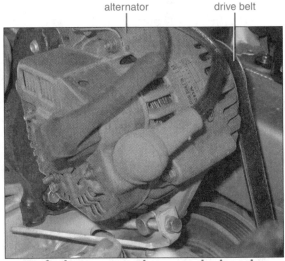

alternator   drive belt

To find your car's alternator, look to the engine belts on the engine front. Alternators are components that are replaced, not repaired, by the do-it-yourselfer.

Working with the Car Computer

Of course, you won't be working *on* your car's *computer*—only *with* it. Actually, there's much your car's computer can tell you without ever touching it. That is, *if* you know how to talk with it.

Car Lingo

A car's **computer** is an electrical device that can read reports from sensors at various locations on the car and respond appropriately. Specific instructions are programmed into the computer at the factory. In addition, code readers are available that can help you learn what the computer knows and how it responds.

So what is it that your car's computer does? It sends out signals to and receives signals from sensors installed throughout your car. These sensors read and adjust fuel, air, spark, emissions, temperatures, and just about everything else going on. In fact, a car computer is more accurately called an engine management computer, computer command control system, or engine control computer.

Your car's owner's manual or service manual will tell you where the car's computer is and how to access it. Some car computers allow you to read diagnostic test results. Others tell you only if something goes wrong. Some require only that you turn the ignition key to "on" and perform some type of ritual (press this button while holding your ear lobe!) to have data displayed on the control console. Others require that you plug in a special electronic tool that reads and interprets the computer's data for you.

For example, one popular diagnostics unit ($200 to $400) can read computer codes on nearly all 1996 and newer cars. (It also covers some earlier models.) It has adapters to plug into the car's computer to read these codes:

◆ Diagnostic trouble codes (DTC)

◆ Generic engine codes (PO)

◆ Emission codes (PI)

◆ Tomorrow's lunch special at your favorite diner (Kidding!)

The codes aren't much good without an interpreter, which can be the car's service or technical manual or an after-market book. Just make sure it covers *your* car, including the engine, transmission, and other specifications.

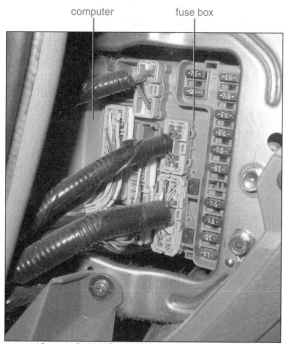

The onboard computer for this car is located behind the fuse boxes and underneath the dashboard.

Here's a look inside an older-style automotive computer; the newer ones are more compact.

Radio and Sound System Repairs

Car radios and sound systems, too, are complex electronic devices. So most repairs mean replacement. However, before you start ripping up the dashboard, here are some things you can do to troubleshoot a car's sound system:

◆ Make a note of the *exact* symptoms (radio doesn't come on, left speaker doesn't work, sound is muffled), because they often suggest the actual problem and solution.

◆ If the radio is on, but no lights or LED indicators are on, check the radio's fuse (either in the car's fuse box or on the power wire to the radio and under the dashboard).

◆ If there's power to the radio, but no sound comes out, first twiddle with the knobs to see if something is incorrectly set.

◆ If there's no sound, check the speaker connection on the side or rear of the radio.

◆ If there's no sound coming through the speakers, check the connection behind the quiet speaker by removing the speaker grill and speaker or by removing part of the car's interior if needed.

◆ If the sound from a specific speaker is raspy, the speaker cone may be damaged and need replacement.

In most cases, the problem will be a loose connection. However, getting access to the connection may take more time than the actual repair.

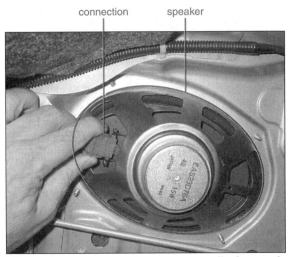

Sound system speakers are usually located in door panels, the dashboard, or under the rear-seat package tray (accessed from the trunk).

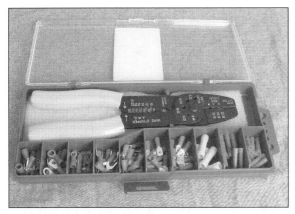

Auto parts stores offer an assortment of electrical tools and connections for installing or rewiring automotive sound systems and other electrical devices.

Solving Other Electrical Problems

What else could go wrong? The most common electrical repair on your car will probably be replacing a light bulb. As with most repairs on the modern (meaning cramped) car, the problem is getting to the part. Some car manufacturers make it relatively easy to replace burned-out bulbs, while others think you should have a mechanic for everything.

Technician's Tip

The filament, the part of the light bulb that glows, is typically the first part of the bulb to fail. Frequently, a bulb doesn't glow because the connection to the car is loose. Carefully turning a bulb (be careful not to break the bulb's glass) may solve the problem.

Of course, check the car's fuses first to see if the fuse is blown. This is especially true if more than one light is out at the same time.

Access to the headlights on many modern cars is from behind the light, from inside the engine compartment.

In general, most car lights are replaced by removing the front lens or the rear of the light fixture. Taking a few minutes to study the problem should tell you which is the right way. If the lens cover has screws on it, chances are they are for accessing the bulbs. If you can easily see the rear of the light fixture and it has a boot where the power wire comes in, carefully removing the boot may yield the bulb as well.

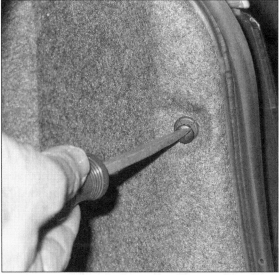

Accessing rear lights typically requires that you remove a cover panel from inside the trunk.

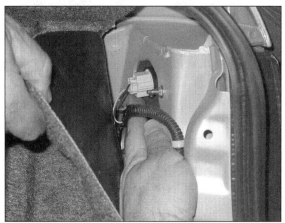

Once the panel is open, unplug the wiring harness. The bulb is probably on the end of the harness.

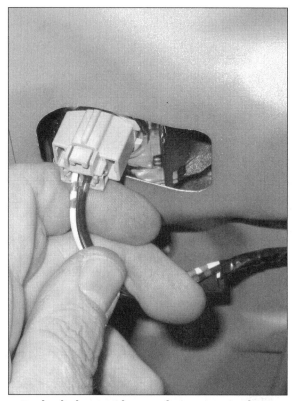

Brake lights on the trunk or rear package deck (behind the rear seat) are accessed from inside the trunk.

You can perform dozens of other electrical tests and repairs using the VOM introduced earlier in this chapter. Because modern cars are 12 volts DC, make sure you set the scale to a higher range (such as 20 volts DC) before testing. And don't forget to use the ohmmeter part of the VOM to determine whether a specific part intended to conduct electricity actually will. Basic instructions come with a new VOM.

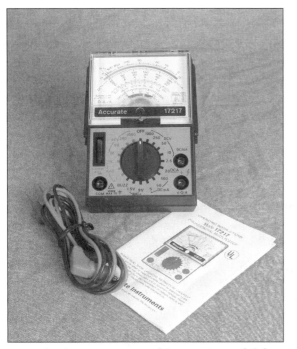

A volt-ohmmeter or multimeter is useful for electrical troubleshooting, but don't test resistance (ohms) on a circuit that has power. Read and follow the VOM's instructions.

The Finish Line

◆ Fuses are the first thing to go in an electrical circuit—and the easiest to test and replace.

◆ You can replace your car's battery in a few minutes with simple tools.

◆ It's much more cost-effective to replace rather than repair an alternator.

◆ There are dozens of electrical components in your car that you can test with a volt-ohmmeter and replace if needed.

Start Your Engines ...

- ◆ How to keep your car looking better longer
- ◆ Touching up body scratches
- ◆ Fixing a body panel so it looks like new
- ◆ Repairing chips in the windshield

Chapter 13

Easy Body Repairs

Whether you want to sell your car for the highest dollar, want to increase pride of ownership, or just want to boost your car's morale, there are many easy car body repairs you can do yourself.

This chapter offers ideas and tips from the pros on how to repair or replace a body panel, touch up your car's paint, and repair or replace a cracked window. Chances are, you can do these jobs yourself. But if you decide not to, at least you'll know how it's done.

Repairing a Body Panel

Today's cars are built differently from their fathers and grandfathers. Older cars used thick metal body components (doors, fenders, bumpers) to minimize damage from impact. Today's cars are built with a sturdy frame (called unibody construction) onto which *body panels* are hung for decoration. Today's cars are actually safer in the event of an accident, but these body panels don't take much abuse. (In fact, just leaning on some cars can dent the body!)

Car Lingo

A **body panel** is a removable component of the car's body. Common body panels include front fenders and rear quarter panels, as well as bumpers, hood, trunk, roof, and doors. (The exterior surface of a door or other moving component is sometimes referred to as the skin.) Body panels are typically constructed of metal or plastic.

Eventually, someone else's car is going to bump, slam, scratch, or roll into your car's body. If the damage is a deep scratch, you can try applying a metal rubbing compound (available from your trusty auto parts store) to make it look less noticeable. You'll be amazed at what it can do! (If you need to touch up the paint, see that section later in this chapter.)

A rubbing compound removes many scratches.

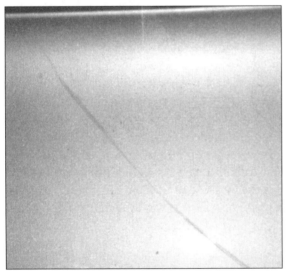

Frequently, surface scratches like this one can easily be repaired with popular auto body products.

Once the compound removes the scratch, clean the area and protect it with a wax.

The scratch is gone!

If the damage is a dent, there are things you can do to save some money by repairing it yourself. Here's how to remove a car body dent:

1. First analyze the dented area. Is it metal or plastic? If it's plastic or some thinner metal, you may be able to carefully push the dent out from the back side with your hand or a rubber hammer. Your auto parts store also sells inexpensive suction cups that can be used to pull the dent out from the front. More stubborn dents will require a dent puller. Ask at your auto store.

2. The pulled dent will need additional filling to be smooth. There is a variety of body filler products available for sanding, filling, and finishing dented metal and plastic auto bodies. The best tip is to read and follow the instructions on the filler container. The store clerk can also advise you and help you select related tools.

sanding block and paper

body file

Common parts for pulling dents, filling dents, and resurfacing body panels.

3. To fill holes and finish repairing a dent, use a file or grinder to remove paint from the area, then use filler to contour. Plastic filler, such as that manufactured under the Bondo trademark, is popular because it's easy to use.

4. To repaint the area, buy matching paint at an auto paint store. If the car is relatively new and not oxidized or faded, you should be able to match the color closely. Apply a primer paint before painting, and smooth the surface with fine sandpaper. If it is oxidized, consider having a painter do the job for you, especially if the damaged area will show.

5. If you're repainting, follow the paint manufacturer's directions. If the exact color isn't available in a pressurized spray can, you can rent an automotive sprayer at a rent-everything store and follow its directions.

Fillers, paints, and metal treatments for body work available at auto parts stores.

Some popular products for removing surface scratches and bugs, and for cleaning car bodies.

Replacing a Body Panel

Sometimes the smartest thing to do is to replace the body panel. This is especially true when the damaged part is a corner fender or front or rear bumper. You can buy these components from larger auto parts stores (although they probably won't be in stock and will need to be ordered). The part may even be available already painted in your car's color from a new car dealer's parts shop or from larger auto parts stores. You can also buy the replacement component through an automotive recycling center (previously known as a junkyard).

Technician's Tip

Your car's service manual may have a parts drawing or list for your car with its body parts and the corresponding numbers. You'll need the parts number to order it. (You don't want to order a left rear fender and receive a new hood!)

Can you replace a body panel yourself? Probably. The key to replacing body panels is figuring out what type of fasteners the manufacturer used to install it. Depending on the component, it may be installed with sheet-metal screws, bolts and nuts, clips, or other fasteners. A door, for example, is hung on hinges attached to the body with large screws. Fenders often use clips that are accessed from inside the engine compartment or the trunk. Bumpers may use bolts and screws for primary support and clips for secondary support. If the service manual is no help, speak with an auto paint store clerk or hire an auto body mechanic to advise you.

A body panel, such as this fender, can be removed by first loosening bolts at the edge of the engine compartment.

Various car brands have their own style and type of body fastener. Fortunately, larger auto parts stores sell a wide variety of fasteners. Find a clerk who knows body parts to make the correct selection.

Here's what a car looks like without the fender.

Touching Up Paint

Maybe the metal or plastic isn't damaged; just the *paint*. It's a deep scratch or blister where paint has been removed. Can you touch it up? As the Three Stooges' Curly Joe would say, "Soitenly!"

mixing jar

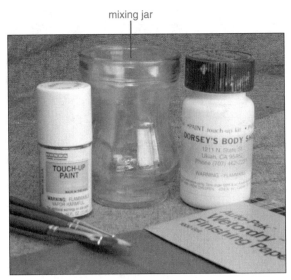

Touching up the paint on a car is relatively easy and requires only basic tools. Make sure you get the correct color to match your car.

 Car Lingo

Automotive **paint** is typically applied in three coats at the factory. The first coat is a primer, the second is the finish coat, and the third is a protective layer called the clear coat. If repairing or replacing your car's paint, make sure you know if a protective clear coat is required. Your auto parts or auto paint store can tell you.

Here's how to do it:

1. Carefully smooth the edge of the scratch or blister with a sanding pen so there are no rough edges.

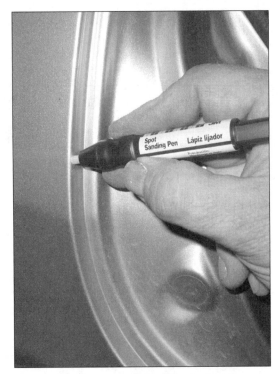

Smaller spots can be sanded with a sanding pen that's easier to control than a small sheet of sandpaper.

2. Fill the crack up to or above the surface of surrounding paint. Large cracks will require plastic filler. Smaller cracks can be filled with primer paint or even a first coat of the finish paint.

3. Sand the area so that the surface is even and smooth. Then apply the primer and final paint, or just the final paint depending on the size of the crack.

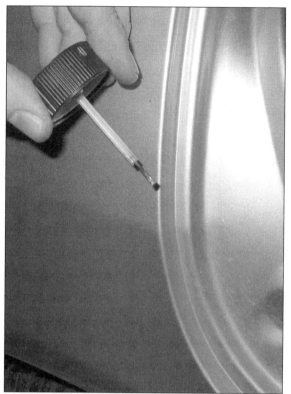

Carefully apply the touch-up paint with a small brush or applicator top.

4. Most modern cars use a protective clear paint called clear coat. If your car's service manual (or auto paint store clerk) recommends clear coat, apply it last following directions on the container.

New cars often come with a small container of touch-up paint. If yours doesn't have one and it is painted a factory color, you may be able to purchase touch-up paint from a new car dealer. Often, the paint color is identified by a code on a label inside the driver's door jamb. If not, the parts counter can help you identify it.

Repairing a Chip in the Windshield

Small stones and other debris traveling at 65 miles an hour can chip your car's windshield. Fortunately, the safety glass used in modern car windows can withstand the shock without shattering. However, the crack weakens the window's strength and may continue to crack until it is replaced.

To repair a windshield chip or a small crack, purchase a windshield chip repair kit at an auto parts store and follow directions on the package.

You can purchase a windshield chip repair kit at most auto parts stores.

In most cases, this means …

1. Clean the windshield with glass cleaner and dry it completely.

2. Apply the adhesive disc over the chip.

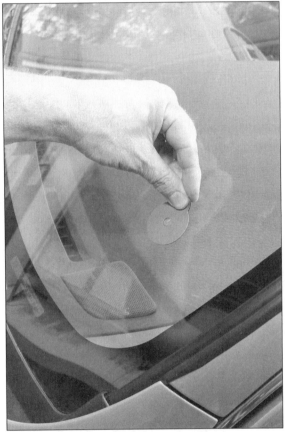

Install the disc over the windshield chip or crack.

3. Place the plastic pedestal or dam atop the disc.

Install the pedestal and dam.

4. Insert the applicator syringe that contains the liquid plastic filler.

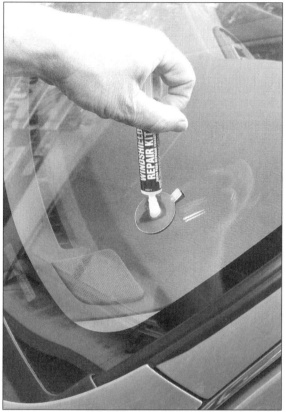

Install the applicator.

5. Push on the applicator to force plastic filler into the chipped area, stopping when filled.

6. Allow the plastic to harden before removing the applicator, pedestal, and disc.

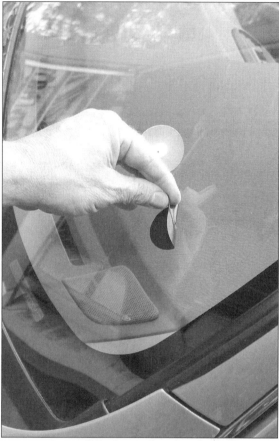

Once the plastic has hardened, remove the components.

You've finished repairing the exterior of your car. The next and final chapter covers the interior.

The Finish Line

◆ Body panels are actually decorative parts that attach to the car's skeleton.

◆ Replacing a body panel can be done with basic tools.

◆ The most difficult part of touch-up painting is matching the color.

◆ You can repair a windshield chip or small crack with a do-it-yourself kit from an auto parts store.

Start Your Engines ...

- ◆ How to clean and repair car upholstery
- ◆ Replacing bigger interior parts
- ◆ Removing interior seats and door panels
- ◆ Fixing your car's seals

Chapter **14**

Easy Interior Repairs

Car interiors get lots of use—and abuse. If your car's interior looks like the home of an emotionally disturbed gorilla, this chapter can help. Taking care of the interior can also help you keep your nice car nicer.

In the coming pages, you'll learn how to repair upholstery and remove stains. You'll also see how to remove and replace interior components such as seats, panels, console, and even the dashboard. Why would you want to? Because (a) the component is damaged and needs replacement, or (b) someone dropped the car keys or a credit card into a crevice between components.

Cleaning Upholstery

What with shuttling around kids and pets and other treasures, your car's upholstery will eventually become stained. It may be grape juice or crayon or special sauce or … uh, never mind. Here's how to get the upholstery looking like (nearly) new again:

1. Identify the stain. Is it greasy, chemical, bio-matter, ink, or what?

2. Identify the upholstery fabric. Is it vinyl, leather, cloth, plastic, or what? Note that some "leather interiors" are actually only leather on the seating surfaces and mock leather everywhere else.

3. Use a brush or clean rag to remove as much of the stain as possible without making it worse.

4. Visit your favorite auto parts store for recommendations and products to remove stain X from surface Y. There are numerous leather cleaners available, so look for one made specifically for leather upholstery and use a leather conditioner when done. The same goes for fabric and vinyl.

Common upholstery cleaning products.

5. If the designated cleaner doesn't work, carefully try one of your household cleaners. Tough stains may require one of the citrus-based cleaners as seen on TV. Test the cleaner on the least conspicuous location in case it discolors the fabric.

6. Once you've identified a cleaner that works on your car's interior, write the product information in your Car Journal. Next month or year you may need it again!

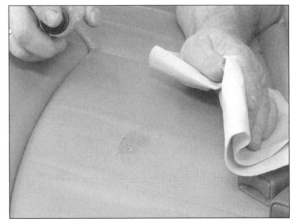

Use the upholstery cleaner following directions on the container.

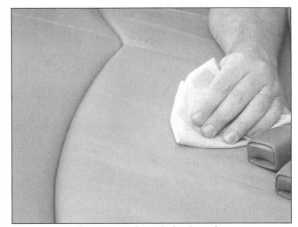

For best results, dab the cleaner away, don't smear.

Repairing Upholstery

Upholstery can be torn, ripped, cut, or come apart at the seams. What to do?

1. Identify the upholstery material.

2. Identify the damage. If it's a rip or cut, can it be repaired by placing repair tape on the underside of the fabric? If a seam has opened, can it be repaired from the underside or should a complementary-colored tape be used to keep it from fraying? Upholstery repair kits available at auto parts stores will tell you what you can and cannot do with them.

3. If necessary, remove the damaged seat or panel from the car and disassemble to repair. Removal instructions follow.

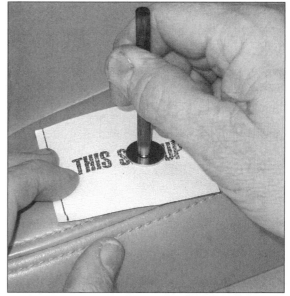

Use the texture pad to duplicate the upholstery's original texture and make the patch look seamless.

Carefully mix the repair material, matching the color of your upholstery.

Replacing a Seat

Sometimes the best way to repair an interior is to remove and disassemble or replace a car seat. How is that done? Of course, exact instructions depends on whether your car has bucket or bench seats and how the manufacturer designed them to be removed. Fortunately, most seats are removed and reinstalled in *about* the same manner.

Technician's Tip

Seat belts and other safety restraints can become twisted in their mechanism, making them difficult to retract or withdraw. If necessary, remove the protective cover on the belt's retracting mechanism and rethread. Also, carefully add a drop or two of light (5-weight) oil every year or two to keep the mechanism working smoothly. While you're at it, add a couple of drops to the belt latches.

To remove bucket-style seats ...

1. Slide the seat forward on its track and remove the bolts that attach the track to the car's floor.

bucket seat track

Move the bucket seat forward to access and remove the track.

2. Slide the seat rearward and remove the attaching bolts.

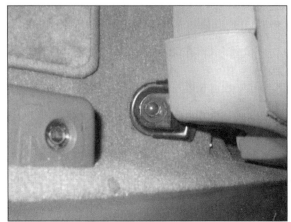

Move the seat back to find the front track connection.

3. Lift the seat to access and disconnect the seat electrical connectors.
4. Carefully remove the seat from the car.
5. If needed, turn the seat over on a protected surface and determine how the seat fabric is attached to the frame. Tools are available through larger auto parts stores for upholstery removal and replacement. (If the seat is powered, the motor will be located in the lower half of the seat.)

To remove bench-style rear seats ...

1. Tip the seat back forward, if possible, to expose pivot brackets located at the back corners of the seat.
2. Remove bolts holding the seat back to the pivot bracket and remove the seat back from the car.
3. Remove bolts holding the seat cushion to the pivot bracket and remove the cushion from the car.

Alternatively, some cars require that you lift up on the front of the cushion (lower) seat and pull toward the front of the car, then lift the back (upper) seat toward the roof. Both units are held in place by clips. Some have additional supports, screws, or bolts.

Most rear seats can be removed by lifting them from the retaining track.

Once out of the car, you can repair or replace the seat as a unit. You can hire an auto reupholsterer to do the work, purchase a new seat through larger auto parts stores, or buy a used one in better condition from an automotive wrecking yard.

Repairing the Console

The majority of modern cars have replaced front bench seats with bucket-style seats with a console between them. The console has become a necessity, housing everything from automatic transmission controls to the parking brake mechanism to a CD holder.

Because most consoles are made of plastic, sometimes covered with vinyl or cloth fabric, they typically aren't repaired. They are replaced. More often, they are removed to access heating or ventilation ducts, the parking brake, a wiring harness that runs to the back of the car, or other important stuff. Many folks need to move the console to wire in new audio speakers or a CD changer in the trunk. Here's how:

1. Open the armrest or otherwise gain access to the rear of the console. Look for screws, clips, and fastener covers that indicate what will need to be removed.

2. Unfasten the console from the floor by loosening bolts, screws, or other fasteners. If there is a parking brake, lift the handle to get it out of the way. If there is an automatic transmission shifter, you may need to remove the T-handle at the top (usually held in place by a set screw).

3. Carefully lift the console, looking for wire harnesses (groups) and plugs. Mark and unplug harnesses as needed to remove the console.

 Auto Alert

Make careful notes indicating which bolts and screws went where, especially if you won't be reinstalling the console for awhile. You'll be thankful you did!

fasteners

Center consoles typically have fasteners at the front and rear.

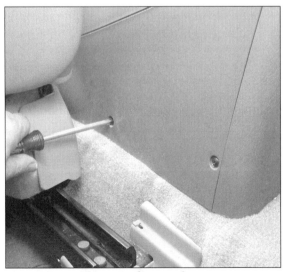

Move the seat forward to access the rear console fasteners.

Removing Door Panels

If you need to replace a door window or motor, repair door damage, or fix a door handle or lock, you may need to remove a door panel—the interior covering of a car's door. Behind it lies the mechanism for raising and lowering windows and unlatching the door so it can be opened. Because there are so many types of cars, I can give you only general tips that will help you remove *most* doors. Here they are:

◆ Door trim is designed to be installed quickly in a factory, so most fasteners will be simple and easy to reach.

◆ Many door panels are fastened at the top of the door below the window with easily removed screws.

◆ Some door panels are held in place with a clip that lines up with and is pressed into a hole in the door, especially around the lower edges of the door; get a panel removal tool from your auto parts store.

◆ Window cranks (called regulator handles) can be removed with a special tool (available at larger auto parts stores) that removes and installs a clip wire located behind the handle itself.

◆ Many cars require that you unscrew the door latch button before removing the door trim.

◆ Recessed door handle compartments typically have a screw cover that can be removed with a small flat screwdriver or special tool to access the screw head.

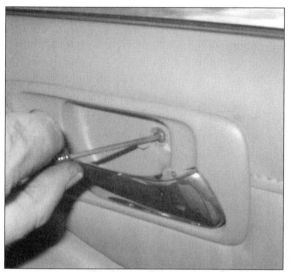

Door panels typically have fasteners located behind covers and trim.

trim fasteners

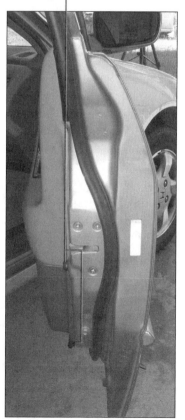

Door panels may also have fasteners or clips at the door's edge.

Removing the Dashboard

I'm going to show you how to remove the *dashboard* from your car—but I'm also going to warn you that this job is usually a project for pros. A dashboard houses the car's computer, electrical, heating and air conditioning, entertainment, and dozens of other vital car systems. You should remove the dashboard only if you know exactly what you need to do (replace a broken instrument cluster) and how to do it, as described in the car's service manual.

> **Car Lingo**
>
> A car's **dashboard** or "dash" is the group of components that stretches across the front of the passenger compartment below the windshield. It includes the instrument panel as well as other controls and systems. The term originally referred to the board or panel on a wagon that kept the horse's hooves and road dirt from dashing or striking the driver.

In general, the dashboard is removed thus:

1. Disconnect the electrical system (typically, disconnect the negative battery lead) and disable the Supplemental Restraint System (SRS), or air bags, as suggested by the car's manufacturer.

2. As needed, remove the radio, disconnecting the wiring harness and antenna lead. Mark any loosened wire connections so you know how to reconnect them later (trust me, they will all begin to look alike).

3. Remove the console (as detailed earlier), glove box (loosen the screws on the back of the door), and any plastic covers under the dashboard.

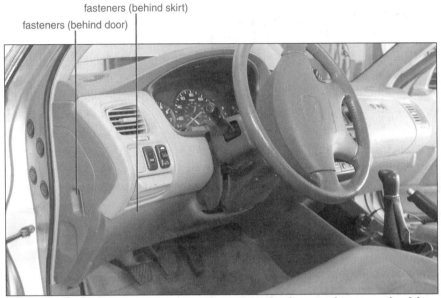

fasteners (behind skirt)

fasteners (behind door)

Dashboards are removed by first removing the lower skirt attached by fasteners at the edges, then loosening fasteners on the dash frame.

4. As needed, remove any trim around the instrument panel to uncover and unscrew fasteners. Carefully pull the instrument panel toward you to expose the rear of specific instruments for replacement.

5. As needed, remove covers from around the steering column and disconnect the wiring harness for the horn, cruise control, and air bag. If you need to remove the steering column, look for and unfasten the bracket that holds the column to the dashboard frame.

6. Pray that you can get it all back together! (Making careful notes will help.)

Replacing Weatherstripping

There's one more job you can do yourself, although it actually qualifies as an exterior-interior job. It's replacing weatherstripping. Weatherstripping is the rubberlike gasket that seals around doors, windows, sunroof, and trunk openings to keep moisture out.

It's a good idea to inspect your car's weatherstripping once a year for damage or wear and replace as needed. If it's brittle or damaged, it can let water in to ruin upholstery or anything stored in the car's trunk. Here's how to replace weatherstripping:

1. Find replacement parts. Your car's service or technical manual can help you identify which part is needed and the part number. For many applications, generic weatherstripping of a specific design and dimension will do fine. You can find this in an auto parts store. Otherwise, you may need to visit the dealership's parts department for an exact replacement.

2. Carefully remove the old weatherstripping so that nothing else is damaged and the new part can easily be put on. Weatherstripping is installed with fasteners, clips, special glue, or a combination of these.

3. Clean the surface to make sure that the new weatherstripping will fit tightly. If you're using new weatherstripping adhesive, follow the manufacturer's recommendations for cleaning and preparing the surface.

4. Test the installation without adhesive or fasteners to make sure the weatherstripping will go on easily and is the correct size.

5. Install the weatherstripping with adhesive and fasteners as needed. Allow the adhesive to dry as recommended by the manufacturer before using the weatherstripping (such as closing the door).

weatherstripping

Weatherstripping around doors is easy to replace if you have the proper tools, adhesives, and replacement parts. Ask your auto parts clerk.

A Clean, Mean Driving Machine

Who cares what the interior of your car looks like? Actually, you should—if you're planning to resell it. Cleaned and repaired interiors sell much faster than dirty ones. Just take a look at any car lot to see what a little vinyl cleaner and an upholstery repair kit can do to the perceived value of a car. In addition, driving a car that's in good condition inside is more pleasurable. Fortunately, it doesn't take much time or money for most interior repairs.

That covers it! You now know how your car runs, how to keep it running longer (and keep it looking good while it runs), and what to do if it doesn't. Thank you for allowing me to share with you. Take care!

The Finish Line

◆ Upholstery cleaning is easy—if you have the right products and tools.

◆ You can replace a damaged seat with a new one with basic tools.

◆ Door panels are designed to be installed—not uninstalled—easily.

◆ If damaged or coming loose, your car's weatherstripping can be replaced with parts from your parts store.

Appendix **A**

Illustrated Car Care and Repair Glossary

advance   Setting the ignition timing so that a spark occurs earlier in the engine's cycle for more efficient operation.

air bag   A restraint system that inflates a hidden bag (or bags) when a sensor at the front of the car is hit in a collision.

air cleaner   A metal or plastic housing on or near the carburetor or fuel injection intake with a filter to remove larger particles from the air.

Air cleaner filter.

alignment   An adjustment to keep parts in the correct relative position, such as the alignment of a car's wheels.

alternator   A component that converts mechanical energy into alternating current (AC) that then must be changed (rectified) into direct current (DC) for use by the car's electrical system.

Alternator (front).

Alternator (rear).

ammeter   An instrument that measures and reports the flow of electric current.

antifreeze   A liquid added to water and used to keep a car's engine cool when running; the antifreeze ingredient keeps the coolant from freezing in cold weather.

antilock brake system (ABS)   An electronic system that controls hydraulics to evenly distribute a car's braking power to avoid skidding. See also *hydraulic.*

Antilock brake system.

automatic choke   A device that reduces airflow into a carburetor when the engine is cold to increase the richness of the fuel/air mixture and help the engine start faster.

automatic transmission   A device that automatically selects gears based on the car's weight and speed.

Automatic transmission.

ball joint   A ball and socket, similar to a joint in a human body, used as a joint in the steering arm.

battery   A device that produces and stores direct current (DC) by converting chemical energy into electrical energy.

Battery.

bearing   A metal part designed to reduce friction between surfaces.

bell housing   A metal shroud that covers the engine's flywheel and the transmission's clutch or torque converter mechanisms. See also *clutch, flywheel,* and *torque converter.*

Bell housing.

bias tire   A tire with cords or layers set at an angle, found on older cars.

body filler   A hardening plastic material used to fill small dents and creases in an auto body.

Body filler.

bore   The width of an engine's cylinder.

cylinder bore

Cylinder bore.

brake   A device that converts kinetic energy into heat energy, slowing down the car.

brake caliper   The part on a disc brake system that squeezes the disc to make the car slow or stop.

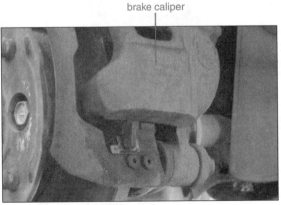

brake caliper

Brake caliper.

brake drum   The part on a drum brake system that receives pressure from the brake shoe. See also *drum brake.*

brake pads   The replaceable surface of a disc brake system's calipers. See also *disc brake.*

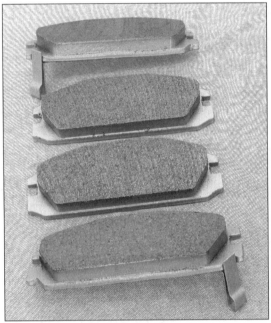

Brake pads.

brake shoe   The movable part of a drum brake system that applies pressure against the brake drum; the replaceable surface of a drum brake system is the friction lining on the shoe.

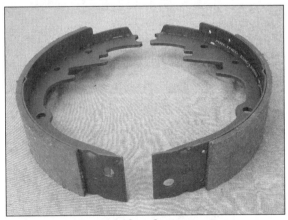

Brake shoes.

breaker-point ignition   An ignition system using two contact points that are moved to interrupt the electrical current within a breaker-point or mechanical distributor, common in older cars.

BTDC (before top dead center)   Any point during the upward movement of an engine piston between the bottom and top.

cam   Also known as a *camshaft*.

camber   The inward or outward tilt of a car's wheel.

camshaft   The rotating shaft inside the engine that opens and closes valves using cam lobes or elliptical sections.

carburetor   A device that dumps a stream of fuel into passing air for distribution to the engine's cylinders for burning.

Carburetor.

caster   The backward or forward tilt of a car's front wheel axle or spindle.

catalytic converter   An exhaust system component that changes pollutants into less harmful elements.

CID (cubic inch displacement)   The total volume of all combustion chambers in an engine measured in cubic inches. To translate engine size from liters to cubic inches, multiply liters by 61.027.

clutch   A device that connects and disconnects the engine from the transmission, or an air conditioner compressor pulley from the compressor shaft.

combustion chamber   The area within an engine cylinder where combustion of a fuel/air mixture takes place.

combustion chamber

Combustion chamber.

compression ratio   The ratio between the space in a cylinder when a piston is at the bottom of its travel and when it's at the top of its travel.

connecting rod   The rod that connects an engine's crankshaft to a piston. See also *crankshaft*.

constant velocity (CV) joint   A joint in a car's driveline that enables the shaft to pivot without vibration. See also *driveline*.

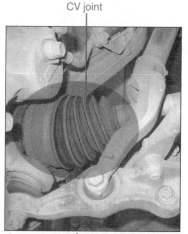
CV joint

Constant velocity (CV) joint.

coolant A mixture of water and ethylene glycol in a car's radiator that helps transfer the engine's heat to the air.

cooling system The system that removes heat from the engine.

crankcase The lowest part of an engine, surrounding the crankshaft.

oil crankcase (rear-wheel drive car)

Crankcase.

crankshaft The main rotating part of an engine that turns the piston's up-and-down motion into a circular motion that can be used by the transmission and, eventually, the wheels.

crankshaft

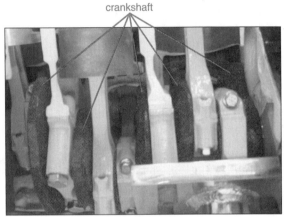

Crankshaft.

cylinder block The largest part of the engine, including cylinders, oil passages, water jackets, and some other components.

cylinder head The detachable part of the engine above the cylinders, sometimes including the valves or other components. Also known as a *head* or *engine head*.

differential The part of a rear-wheel-drive system that uses gears to transfer the driveline's power to two wheels as needed. See also *driveline*.

Differential.

disc brake   A brake system that applies caliper pressure against a disc on wheels to stop the car. Typically used in the front wheels of many cars.

Disc brake.

distributor   A device that sends the coil's electricity evenly and at precisely the right time to the engine's spark plugs.

Distributor.

double-overhead cam (DOHC) engine
An engine that uses two camshafts to control valves—one for the intake valves and one for the exhaust valves.

drive belt   The rubber and fabric belts that apply the crankshaft pulley's rotation to rotate an alternator, water pump, power steering pump, and air conditioning compressor, if so equipped. Some cars use a single belt, called a serpentine drive belt, for driving many components.

drive shaft   The long hollow tube with universal joints at each end that transfers power from the transmission to the differential.

drive train   All components that transmit power to a car's wheels, including the clutch or torque converter, transmission, drive shaft, joints, and the differential or drive axle.

driveline   Universal joint, drive shaft, and related parts that connect the transmission with the driving axles.

drum brake   A brake system that applies brake shoes against the inside of a brake drum to stop or slow a car.

Drum brake.

electrical system   The components that start your car, replenish and store electricity, and operate electrical devices.

electrolyte   Sulfuric acid and water solution within a car battery that produces electricity.

electronic fuel injection (EFI) A computer-controlled system that injects fuel into engine cylinders.

electronic ignition An automotive ignition system that uses electronic signals to interrupt the electrical voltage within the distributor—common in cars built since 1976.

engine head See *cylinder head*.

exhaust emission control One or more devices for reducing the engine's contaminants before they go into the atmosphere.

exhaust gas recirculation (EGR) system A system that recirculates exhaust gases to lower engine combustion temperatures and reduce nitrogen oxides.

exhaust manifold A system that collects exhaust gases from the cylinders and delivers them to the exhaust pipes.

filter A replaceable part that attempts to keep contaminants out of the air, fuel, or oil used by an engine.

flathead An engine with the valves in the engine block so the engine's head is flat.

flywheel A round metal wheel at the end of the crankshaft that collects and passes the engine's power to the transmission.

four-wheel drive A drive system that distributes the engine's power to all four wheels.

freon-12 A fluorocarbon refrigerant once used in automotive air conditioning systems; now banned as a hazard to the earth's ozone layer.

front-wheel drive A drive system that distributes the engine's power to the wheels at the front of the vehicle.

fuel Any combustible substance that is burned to provide power or heat—for example, gasoline, ethanol, methanol, diesel, natural gas, or propane.

fuel/air mixture The combustible mixture of gasoline fuel, and air fed to an automobile engine.

fuel filter A replaceable part that attempts to keep contaminants out of the fuel used by an engine.

Fuel filter.

fuel injection Injects metered fuel into the intake manifold at each cylinder for burning.

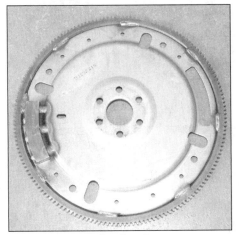

Flywheel.

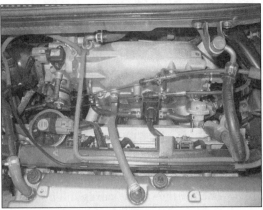

Fuel injection.

fuel pump   A device that draws fuel from a tank and delivers it to the fuel system.

Fuel pump (cutaway).

fuse   The weakest link in an electrical circuit, designed to fail first before an electrical overload damages other components, removed from the *fuse panel* with a *fuse puller*.

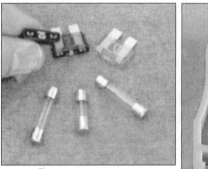

Fuse assortment.

Fuse puller.

fuse panel   A panel where electrical fuses are mounted for easy access.

gap   Typically, the distance a spark must jump between the center electrode and the ground electrode on a spark plug.

gasket   A thin, pliable material used as a seal between two metal surfaces.

Gaskets.

gasoline   The most common fuel used to power automobiles; refined from petroleum.

generator   A device that converts mechanical energy into alternating current (AC) that then is changed to direct current (DC) for use by the car's electrical system.

ground   The neutral side of an automotive electrical system, typically the negative terminal, that is attached (grounded) to the engine or frame.

head   See *cylinder head*.

horsepower   A confusing formula for determining the power generated by an engine.

hydraulic   A system that uses hydraulic oil to transmit or magnify power.

hydrocarbons   Any compound that has hydrogen and carbon molecules, such as gasoline, diesel, or other petroleum products.

idle system   The system within a carburetor that maintains an even flow of fuel when the engine is running but the car isn't moving.

ignition coil   An electromagnetic device in a car that converts low voltage into high voltage.

ignition system   The system that supplies and distributes the spark needed for combustion within the engine.

independent suspension   A suspension system that allows two wheels on the same axle to move independently.

intake manifold   A system that distributes air or a fuel-and-air mixture to the engine's cylinders.

internal combustion   The combustion or burning of fuel in an enclosed area, such as an engine's combustion chamber.

kickdown   A switch or linkage that moves an automatic transmission into a lower gear when the accelerator pedal is pushed down.

leaf spring   A group of flat steel springs in a car's suspension system used to minimize up-and-down motion.

lifter   The metal part of a valve system between the cam lobe and the push rod or rocker arm. See also *camshaft*.

liter   A measurement of volume equal to 61.027 cubic inches. To translate engine size in cubic inches to liters, multiply cubic inches by .0164.

lubrication system   The engine passages, the oil pump and filter, and related parts that lubricate the engine to reduce wear on moving parts.

MacPherson strut   A component found on most front-wheel-drive cars that combines a suspension coil spring and shock absorber in one unit. See also *shock absorber* and *suspension*.

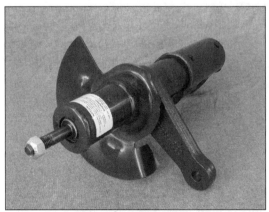

MacPherson strut.

manual steering   An automotive steering system that doesn't use a power booster.

manual transmission   A transmission that requires the driver to manually select the operating gear.

master cylinder   A hydraulic cylinder that magnifies the driver's foot pressure to evenly operate the four wheel brakes.

millimeter   A metric measurement equal to .03937 of an inch. There are 25.4 millimeters to an inch.

mixture adjusting screw   A tapered screw that regulates the fuel in a carburetor's airstream.

motor   An electromagnetic device such as a starting motor; technically a car's power source is an engine rather than a motor.

muffler   A part that reduces the sound of automotive exhaust by passing it through baffles and chambers.

octane   A unit of measurement for a fuel's tendency to detonate or knock.

odometer   A meter that reports miles driven since the car was built or since being reset at the beginning of a trip.

OEM (original-equipment manufacturer)   The maker of parts installed on the car when built.

oil pan   The removable part of an engine below the block that serves as a reservoir for the engine's oil.

oil pump   A part that pumps lubricating oil from the oil pan through the engine as needed to minimize wear.

overdrive   A transmission gear designed to reduce engine speed and increase fuel economy when the car is operating at more than 50 miles per hour; some cars use a fifth gear instead of an overdrive gear.

overhead cam (OHC) engine An engine with the camshaft in the cylinder head instead of the engine block.

overhead valve (OHV) engine An engine with the valves in the cylinder head instead of the engine block.

pad wear indicator A device that indicates when brake pads are worked to the point of needing replacement.

parking brake A hand- or foot-operated brake that applies brake shoes or brake pads against the braking surface on a car's rear wheels; also called an emergency brake.

passenger-restraint system A system of seatbelts and interlocks or internal switches designed to protect passengers from injury in an accident.

piston The movable floor of an engine cylinder that is connected by a rod to the crankshaft.

Engine piston.

piston rings The rings that fit around the side of a piston and against the cylinder wall to seal the compression chamber.

pitman-arm steering A steering system popular for 50 years that used a gear to transmit the driver's steering motion to a swiveling component called the pitman arm.

points See *breaker-point ignition.*

positive crankcase ventilation (PCV) A system of pipes and passages that recirculates vapors from the oil pan for burning by the engine.

power brake booster A hydraulic and vacuum unit that helps the brake's master cylinder magnify the driver's foot pressure to evenly operate the four wheel brakes.

power steering A hydraulic unit that magnifies the driver's motion to more easily steer the car.

power train See *drive train.*

push rod A rod that connects the valve lifter to the rocker arm.

rack-and-pinion steering A steering system with one gear across another, making steering more responsive than pitman-arm steering. See also *pitman-arm steering.*

radial tire A tire with cords or layers laid radially or across the tread; the most popular design today.

radiator A car part that reduces engine temperatures by transferring the heat in a liquid (coolant) to the air.

Radiator and hoses.

rear-wheel drive   A drive system that distributes the engine's power to the wheels at the rear of the vehicle.

rocker arm   A part of an overhead valve system that transfers upward motion of the lifters and/or push rod to downward motion of the valves. See also *lifter*.

rod bearing   A smooth metal part between the crankshaft and individual connecting rods for reducing wear.

rotor   (1) A brake disc on a disc brake system; (2) A distributor part that rotates to transmit electricity to each spark plug wire through the distributor cap.

brake rotor

Brake rotor.

shock absorber   A cylinder that uses hydraulic fluid to dampen a wheel's up-and-down movement caused by bumps in the road.

Shock absorber.

single-overhead cam (SOHC)   An engine that uses one camshaft in the engine's head to control both the intake valves and exhaust valves.

sludge   A pasty compound of oil, water, and debris that accumulates in the oil pan and around rocker arms, reducing the flow of oil through the engine. See also *rocker arm*.

spark advance   See *advance*.

spark plug   A metal-and-ceramic part that uses electricity to ignite the fuel/air mixture in the cylinder.

distributor   spark plug wires

Spark plug wires and caps.

speedometer   A meter that indicates a car's speed by measuring the driveline's turning or rotation.

stabilizer bar   A bar linking the suspension systems on two wheels (front or rear) to stabilize steering turning.

starter   An electric motor that engages, spins, and disengages the engine's flywheel in order to start the engine. See also *flywheel*.

Starter motor.

steering column The shaft from the steering wheel to the steering gear.

steering system A system of parts that transfers the turning movements of the steering wheel to the wheels.

steering tie rod

Steering components (including tie rod).

stroke The distance a piston moves up and down within an engine cylinder.

stroke (piston's travel from top to bottom)

Piston stroke.

strut See *MacPherson strut.*

suspension The group of parts (springs, shock absorbers, and so on) that suspends the car's frame and body above the wheels.

thermostat A heat-controlled valve that regulates the flow of coolant in an engine based on a preset minimum temperature.

Thermostat.

tie rod   A jointed rod that ties the steering gear to the wheels.

timing gears   The gears that keep the camshaft (valves) in time with the crankshaft (pistons) using a timing chain or timing belt. See also *camshaft* and *crankshaft*.

torque converter   An automatic clutch on an automatic transmission. See also *differential* and *transmission*.

transaxle   A transmission and differential axle combined into one unit. See also *automatic transmission* and *clutch*.

transmission   A component that transmits the engine's power to the wheels using gears.

tune-up   A periodic adjustment and replacement of parts as recommended by the car's manufacturer.

turbocharger   Uses a turbine to force more air into the cylinders to increase power.

universal joint   A joint in a car's drive shaft that allows the shaft to pivot.

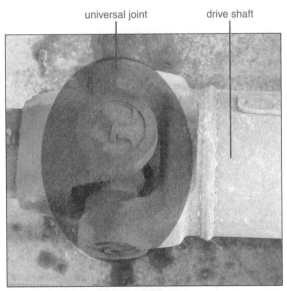

Universal joint.

valve   A part of an engine that opens and closes to control the flow of a liquid, gas, or vacuum. Most commonly, the intake valve lets fuel/air into, and the exhaust valve lets combusted gases out of, an engine's cylinder.

Engine valves in a head.

voltage regulator   A device that regulates or controls the voltage output of an alternator or generator. See also *alternator* and *generator*.

wheel cylinder   A hydraulic cylinder at each wheel that magnifies the master cylinder's pressure to evenly operate the wheel's brake system.

wiring diagram   A drawing depicting the electrical wiring and devices in a car—useful for troubleshooting electrical problems.

zerk fitting   A nipple fitting installed to allow pressurized lubricating grease to be forced into a component.

Car Care and Repair Resources

Auto Magazines Online

AutoWeek Online (www.autoweek.com)

Car and Driver (www.caranddriver.com)

Motor Age (www.motorage.com)

Motor Magazine (www.motor.com/magazine.htm)

Motor Trend Online (www.motortrend.com)

Popular Mechanics Automotive (www.popularmechanics.com/automotive)

Woman Motorist (www.womanmotorist.com)

Buying and Selling Online

AutoTrader (www.autotrader.com) is a used vehicle shopping site with more than 1.5 million listings.

AutoVantage (www.autovantage.com) is a membership new and used car-buying service and a good source of make, model, and price information, including new car summaries.

AutoWeb (www.autoweb.com) has an extensive selection of new and used automotive-related content including purchase information, research, financing, insurance, maintenance, and lots of car reviews, too.

AutoWorld (www.autoworld.com) gathers data daily from nationwide sources, and the database is updated continuously.

Carfax (www.carfax.com), with a database of over 1.4 billion records compiled from over 170 separate sources, provides information on used vehicles. It identifies vehicles with total loss, salvage, flood damage, and theft histories, as well as odometer fraud.

CarPoint (carpoint.msn.com) includes lots of new and used car prices, reviews, shopping guides, interest rate information, and an extensive news and advice section.

Carsdirect (www.carsdirect.com) offers one-stop car buying including selection, financing, and leasing.

Consumer Reports (www.consumerreports.com) includes a wide variety of used and new car information, reports, tips, comparisons, advice, and database search functions.

Consumer Reports Auto Hub (www.consumerreports.org/news/autos) offers information on the magazine's top picks, new and used car buying advice, car care, and driving tips.

Edmund's Buyer's Guide (www.edmunds.com) offers valuation, road tests, buyer's advice, and additional consumer information on new and used cars.

Kelley Blue Book (www.kbb.com) includes new and used car price reports, both retail and trade-in values.

N.A.D.A Used Car Guide (www.nadaguides.com) is the online form of the little orange book published monthly by the National Automobile Dealer's Association.

Yahoo! Autos (autos.yahoo.com) is a compendium of other sites about automobiles.

Maintenance and Repair Online

ALLDATA (www.alldata.com/recalls) provides a list of recalls and technical service bulletins for most cars since 1960. The list can be ordered from ALLDATA by registering online, or check with a mechanic who uses the ALLDATA system.

Automotive Engine Rebuilders Association (www.aera.org) is a trade association for businesses that rebuild automotive engines.

Automotive Service Association (www.asashop.org) is an organization of automotive service businesses.

CanadianDriver (www.canadiandriver.com) is a comprehensive guide to Canadian automotive resources, with over 1,700 links to Canadian automotive websites, including car dealers, parts retailers, automotive services, consumer information, government organizations, and industry associations.

Car Care Council (www.carcarecouncil.org) is a widely respected source of automotive maintenance and repair information established in 1968. The council is a nonprofit organization dedicated to providing motorists with information concerning the importance of vehicle maintenance and repair.

Car Care and Repair on the Road (www.bbb.org/library/carcare.html) offers valuable automotive tips from the Better Business Bureau.

Car Talk (cartalk.cars.com) is Tom and Ray Magliozzi's hilarious and informative National Public Radio program website.

Car Tips (www.pueblo.gsa.gov/cars.html) from the Consumer Information Center of Pueblo, Colorado, includes a safety checklist for your car and tips on changing your own motor oil, with an explanation of why recycling oil helps the environment and saves energy.

CARtimes (www.cartimes.com) is an extensive and easy-to-use automotive website directory dedicated to the automobile and the automotive enthusiast.

JC Whitney (jcwhitney.com) is the largest direct marketer of aftermarket automotive accessories.

National Institute for Automotive Service Excellence (ASE) (www.asecert.org) is the premier group for certifying and training automotive service technicians.

Service Technicians Society (www.sts.sae.org) is affiliated with the Society of Automotive Engineers. This group's aim is to advance the skills, education, and professionalism of service technicians to support excellence in the mobility industry.

Tire Industry Directory (www.tireguides.com/directory.html) is an extensive list of tire manufacturers and other related websites.

Tire Industry Safety Council (www.tisc.org) is a trade association supported by U.S. tire manufacturers to disseminate facts about tire care and safety to consumers. It includes useful information on tire inflation pressure, rotation, inspection, and other tire care tips.

Uniform Tire Quality Grading System (www.nhtsa.dot.gov/cars/testing/tirerate) is a tire information system designed to help buyers make relative comparisons among tires. Under UTQGS, tires are graded by the manufacturers in three areas: treadwear, traction, and temperature resistance.

USCAR (www.uscar.org) is home to the United States Council for Automotive Research, an umbrella organization formed by Chrysler Corporation, Ford Motor Company, and General Motors Corporation to strengthen the technology base of the U.S.

auto industry through cooperative research. Many advanced technologies are now being researched for possible application on cars of the future.

Weekend Mechanics Club (www.weekendmechanicsclub.com) is brought to you by the Automotive Aftermarket Industry Association and its members. Check out its Store Finder, Shop Finder, and Find a Part databases.

Auto Manufacturer Consumer Departments

Acura
Customer Relations Department
1919 Torrance Boulevard 500-2N-7E
Torrance, CA 90501-2746
Toll free: 1-800-382-2238
Toll free: 1-800-594-8500 (roadside assistance)
Fax: 310-783-3535
Website: www.acura.com

Alfa Romeo Distributors of North America, Inc.
7454 Brokerage
Orlando, FL 32809
407-856-5000
Fax: 407-856-5000

American Honda Motor Co., Inc.
Consumer Affairs Department
1919 Torrance Boulevard
Torrance, CA 90501-2746
310-783-2000
Toll free: 1-800-999-1009
Fax: 310-783-3273
Website: www.honda.com

American Honda Motor Co., Inc.
Central Zone 4
Michigan (except for Upper Peninsula),
Indiana, Ohio, Kentucky
Customer Relations Department
101 South Stanfield Road
Troy, OH 45373-8010
Toll free: 1-800-999-1009
Fax: 937-332-1010
Website: www.honda.com

American Honda Motor Co., Inc.
Mid-Atlantic Zone
Customer Relations Department
902 Wind River Lane, Suite 200
Gaithersburg, MD 20878-1974
301-990-2020
Toll free: 1-800-999-1009
Fax: 301-990-6808
Website: www.honda.com

American Honda Motor Co., Inc.
Northwest Zone 2
Washington, Oregon, Idaho, Montana,
Wyoming, North Dakota, South Dakota,
Hawaii, Alaska
Customer Relations Department
12439 NE Airport Way
Portland, OR 97220
503-256-0943
Fax: 503-251-1348
Website: www.honda.com

American Honda Motor Co., Inc.
South Central Zone 3
Texas (excluding El Paso), Arkansas (excluding
Fayetteville, Bentonville, Fort Smith,
Jonesboro), Oklahoma (excluding Lawton,
Ardmore), Louisiana, Mississippi
Customer Relations Department
4525 Royal Lane
Irving, TX 75063-2583
972-929-5481
Fax: 972-929-5403
Website: www.honda.com

American Honda Motor Co., Western Zone
Customer Relations Department
1919 Torrance Boulevard
Torrance, CA 90509-2260
323-781-4565
Website: www.honda.com

American Isuzu Motors, Inc.
Owner Relations Department
13340 183rd Street
Cerritos, CA 90702-6007
Toll free: 1-800-255-6727
Fax: 562-229-5455
Website: www.isuzu.com

American Suzuki Motor Corp.
Customer Relations Department
P.O. Box 1100
3251 East Imperial Highway
Brea, CA 92822-1100
714-996-7040, ext. 380 (motorcycles)
714-572-1490
Toll free: 1-800-934-0934 (automotive only)
Fax: 714-524-2512
Website: www.suzuki.com

Aston Martin, Jaguar, Land Rover Premier
Auto Group
Customer Relations Department
U.S. National Headquarters
1 Premier Place
Irvine, CA 92618
949-341-6100
Toll free: 1-800-452-4827
Fax: 949-341-6152
Website: www.jaguar.com

Audi of America, Inc.
Client Relations
3499 West Hamlin Road
Rochester Hills, MI 48309
Toll free: 1-800-822-2834
Fax: 248-754-6504
Website: www.audiusa.com

BMW of North America, Inc.
Corporate Office
300 Chestnut Ridge Road
Woodcliff Lake, NJ 07675
201-307-4000
Toll free: 1-800-831-1117 (BMW Customer
Service Center)
Fax: 201-930-8362
Website: www.bmwusa.com

Buick Division General Motors Corp.
Customer Assistance Center
P.O. Box 33136
Detroit, MI 48232-5136
313-556-5000
Toll free: 1-800-521-7300
Toll free: 1-800-252-1112 (roadside assistance)
TDD toll free: 1-800-832-8425
Website: www.buick.com

Cadillac Motor Car Division
Customer Assistance Center
P.O. Box 33169
Detroit, MI 48232-5169
Toll free: 1-800-458-8006
Toll free: 1-800-882-1112 (roadside assistance)
TDD toll free: 1-800-833-2622
Website: www.cadillac.com

Chevrolet Motor Division,
General Motors Corp.
Customer Assistance Center
P.O. Box 33170
Detroit, MI 48232-5170
Toll free: 1-800-222-1020
Toll free: 1-800-243-8872 (roadside assistance)
TDD toll free: 1-800-833-2438
Fax: 313-556-5108
Website: www.chevrolet.com

Daihatsu America, Inc.
Consumer Affairs Department
28 Centerpointe Drive, Suite 120
La Palma, CA 90623
714-690-4700
Toll free: 1-800-777-7070
Fax: 714-690-4720
Website: www.daihatsu.com/

Daimler Chrysler Customer Center
P.O. Box 21-8004
Auburn Hills, MI 48321-8004
Toll free: 1-800-992-1997
Fax: 248-512-8084
Website: www.chrysler.com

Ferrari North America, Inc.
Corporate Office
250 Sylvan Avenue
Englewood Cliffs, NJ 07632
201-816-2600
Fax: 201-816-2626
E-mail: administrative@ferrari.com
Website: www.ferrari.com

Ford Dispute Settlement Board
P.O. Box 5120
Southfield, MI 48086-5120
Toll free: 1-800-688-2429

Ford Motor Company
Customer Assistance Center
16800 Executive Plaza Drive
P.O. Box 6248
Dearborn, MI 48121
Toll free: 1-800-392-3673 (all makes)
Toll free: 1-800-521-4140 (Lincoln and
Merkur only)
TDD toll free: 1-800-232-5952
Website: www.ford.com

General Motors Corporation
Corporate Affairs/Community Relations
100 Renaissance Center
Detroit, MI 48265
313-667-3800
313-556-5000

GMC Division, General Motors Corp.
Customer Assistance Center
P.O. Box 33172
Detroit, MI 48232-5172
Toll free: 1-800-462-8782
Toll free: 1-800-223-7799 (roadside assistance)
TDD toll free: 1-800-462-8583
Website: www.gmc.com

Honda
See American Honda Motor Co., Inc.

Hyundai Motor America
Consumer Affairs
10550 Talbert Avenue
P.O. Box 20850
Fountain Valley, CA 92728-0850
714-965-3000
Toll free: 1-800-633-5151
Fax: 714-965-3861
E-mail: cmd@hma.service.com
Website: www.hyundai.usa.com

Isuzu
See American Isuzu Motors, Inc.

Jeep/Eagle Division of Chrysler Corp.
Customer Relations
P.O. Box 21-8004
Auburn Hills, MI 48321
Toll free: 1-800-992-1997
Fax: 248-512-8084

Kia Motors America, Inc.
Consumer Assistance Center
P.O. Box 52410
Irvine, CA 92619-2410
Toll free: 1-800-333-4KIA
Fax: 949-470-2812
Website: www.kia.com

Lexus
A Division of Toyota Motor Sales, U.S.A., Inc.
Customer Satisfaction Department
Mail Drop L203, 19001 South Western
Avenue
Torrance, CA 90509-2732
Toll free: 1-800-25 LEXUS
Fax: 310-468-2992
Website: www.lexus.com

Mazda North American Operations
Corporate Office
Customer Relations Manager
Jamboree Plaza
4 Park Plaza, Suite 1250
Irvine, CA 92614
Toll free: 1-800-222-5500
Website: www.mazdausa.com

Mercedes Benz USA, Inc.
Customer Assistance Center
3 Paragon Drive
Montvale, NJ 07645
Toll free: 1-800-222-0100
Toll free: 1-800-367-6372
(1-800-FOR-MERC)
Fax: 201-476-6213
Website: www.mbusa.com

Mitsubishi Motor Sales of America
Customer Relations
6400 Katella Avenue
Cypress, CA 90630-0064
Toll free: 1-800-MITSU-2000
Website: www.mitsubishimotors.com

Nissan North America, Inc.
Consumer Affairs Group
P.O. Box 191
Gardena, CA 90248-0191
310-532-3111
Toll free: 1-800-647-7261 (all consumer
inquiries)
Fax: 310-771-2025
Website: www.nissan-usa.com

Oldsmobile Division General Motors Corp.
Customer Assistance Network
P.O. Box 33171
Detroit, MI 48232-5171
Toll free: 1-800-442-6537
Toll free: 1-800-535-6537 (roadside assistance)
TDD toll free: 1-800-833-6537
Website: www.oldsmobile.com

Peugeot Motors of America, Inc.
Consumer Relations
Overlook at Great Notch
150 Clove Road
Little Falls, NJ 07424
973-812-4444
Toll free: 1-800-345-5545
Fax: 973-812-2148
E-mail: peugeot2@bellatlantic.net
Website: www.peugeot.com

Pontiac Division, General Motors Corp.
Customer Assistance Center
P.O. Box 33172
Detroit, MI 48232-5172
Toll free: 1-800-762-2737 (1-800-PM-CARES)
Toll free: 1-800-762-3743 (1-800-ROADSIDE)
TDD toll free: 1-800-833-7668
Website: www.gm.com

Porsche Cars North America, Inc.
Owner Relations
980 Hammond Drive, Suite 1000
Atlanta, GA 30328
770-290-3500
Toll free: 1-800-545-8039
Fax: 770-360-3711
Website: www.porsche.com

Saab Cars USA, Inc.
Customer Assistance Center
4405-A International Boulevard
Norcross, GA 30093
770-279-0100
Toll free: 1-800-955-9007
Fax: 770-279-6499
Website: www.saabusa.com

Saturn Corporation, Division of General Motors Corp.
Saturn Customer Assistance Center
100 Saturn Parkway
Spring Hill, TN 37174
931-486-5050
Toll free: 1-800-553-6000
Fax: 931-486-5059
Website: www.saturn.com

Subaru of America, Inc.
National Customer Service Center
Subaru Plaza, P.O. Box 6000
Cherry Hill, NJ 08002
856-488-8500
Toll free: 1-800-782-2783
Fax: 856-488-0485
Website: www.subaru.com

Toyota Motor Sales USA, Inc.
Customer Assistance Center
Department H200
19001 S. Western Avenue
Torrance, CA 90509
310-468-4000
Toll free: 1-800-331-4331
Fax: 310-468-7800
Website: www.toyota.com

Volkswagen of America
Customer Relations
Hills Corporate Center
3499 West Hamlin Road
Rochester Hills, MI 48309
Toll free: 1-800-822-8987 or 1-800-DRIVE VW
Fax: 248-340-4660
Website: www.vw.com

Volvo Cars of North America Corporate Office
Customer Service
P.O. Box 914
7 Volvo Drive, Building A
Rockleigh, NJ 07647-0915
Toll free: 1-800-458-1552
Fax: 201-768-8695
Website: www.volvocars.com

Automotive Dispute Resolution Programs

Center for Auto Safety (CAS)
1825 Connecticut Avenue NW, Suite 330
Washington, DC 20009
202-328-7700, ext. 107
Website: www.autosafety.org

BBB AUTO LINE
Council of Better Business Bureaus, Inc.
4200 Wilson Boulevard, Suite 800
Arlington, VA 22203-1838
703-276-0100
Toll free: 1-800-955-5100
TDD/TTY: 703-276-1862
Fax: 703-525-8277
E-mail: info@cbbb.bbb.org
Website: www.bbb.org

International Association of Lemon Law Administrators
89 Annabessacook Drive
Winthrop, ME 04364
207-377-8752
Fax: 207-377-5992 207-377-8752
E-mail: ialla@ialla.net
Websites: www.ialla.net,
www.TheLemonLaw.org

Motorist Assurance Program
7101 Wisconsin Avenue, Suite 1200
Bethesda, MD 20814
301-634-4954
301-634-4955
Fax: 202-318-0378
E-mail: map@motorist.org
Website: www.motorist.org

National Automobile Dealers Association
8400 Westpark Drive
McLean, VA 22102
703-821-7000
Toll free: 1-800-252-6232
Fax: 703-821-7075
Website: www.nada.org

National Institute for Automotive Service Excellence (ASE)
101 Blue Seal Drive SE, Suite 101
Leesburg, VA 20175
703-669-6600
Website: www.asecert.org

RV Consumer Group
P.O. Box 520
Quilcene, WA 98376
Order Desk: 1-800-405-3325
E-mail: rvgroup@rv.org
Website: www.rv.org

Preventative Maintenance Tips

1. **Check the antifreeze/coolant level weekly.** Some cars have transparent reservoirs with level markings. Fill to the level marking with 50/50 solution of antifreeze and water. Caution: Do not remove the pressure cap when the engine is hot!

2. **Inspect belts and hoses monthly.** Replace worn, glazed, or frayed belts. Tighten them when more than ½" of slack can be depressed between the pulleys. Vehicles with spring-loaded belt tensioners require no adjustment. Replace bulging, rotten, or brittle hoses and tighten the clamps. If a hose looks bad, or feels too soft or too hard, it should be replaced.

3. **Check transmission fluid monthly.** Do this while the engine is warm and running and with the parking brake on. Shift to drive, then to park. Remove the dipstick, wipe it dry, insert it, and remove it again. Add the approved type fluid, if needed. Do not overfill!

4. **Check brake fluid monthly.** First, wipe dirt from the brake master cylinder reservoir lid. Pry off the retainer clip and remove the lid or unscrew the plastic lid, depending on which type your vehicle has. If you need fluid, add the approved type and check for possible leaks throughout the system. Fill to the mark on the reservoir. Caution: Do not overfill!

5. **Check the power steering fluid level once per month.** Simply remove the reservoir dipstick. If the level is down, add fluid and inspect the pump and hoses for leaks.

6. **Check the air filter every other month.** Replace it when it's dirty or as part of a tune-up. It's easy to reach, right under the big metal "lid" in a carbureted engine; or in a rectangular box at the forward end of the air duct hose assembly.

7. **Check oil every other fill-up.** Remove the dipstick and wipe it clean. Insert it fully and remove it again. If it's low, add oil. To maintain peak performance, change oil every 3,000 miles or every three months, whichever comes first. Replace the oil filter with every oil change.

8. **Keep the windshield washer fluid reservoir full.** When topping off, use some windshield washer fluid on a rag to clean off the wiper blades. In winter months, pay attention to the freezing point of the washer fluid.

9. **Check your car's battery with every oil change.** Use extreme caution when handling a battery because it can produce explosive gases. Do not smoke, create a spark, or light a match near a battery, and always wear protective glasses and gloves. Cables should be attached securely and be free of corrosion. If the battery has filler holes, add only clear, odorless drinking water.

10. **Inspect the windshield wiper blades whenever you clean your windshield.** Don't wait until rubber is worn or brittle to replace them! Wiper blades should be replaced at least once per year, and more often if smearing or chattering occurs.

11. **Be sure all of your car's lights are clean and working.** Check brake lights, turn signals, and emergency flashers, too. Keep spare bulbs and fuses in your vehicle.

12. **Keep tires inflated to the recommended pressure and check for tire wear.** It helps if you own your own tire gauge. Check the tires regularly for cuts, bulges, and excessive treadwear. Uneven wear indicates tires are misaligned or out of balance. Keep a record of tire rotation. Rotate at the first 5,000 miles and every 7,500 miles thereafter.

13. **Look for signs of oil seepage on shock absorbers.** Test the shock action by bouncing the car up and down. The car should stop bouncing when you step back. Worn or leaking shocks should be replaced. Always replace shock absorbers in pairs.

14. **Look underneath the car for loose or broken exhaust clamps and supports.** Check for holes in the muffler or pipes. Replace rusted or damaged parts. Have emission checked at least once per year for compliance with local laws.

15. **Take good care** of your car and it will take care of you!

Index

Car Care Journal